Transforming the Pain
A Workbook on Vicarious Traumatization

Also by the Authors

Trauma and the Therapist:
Countertransference and Vicarious Traumatization
in Psychotherapy with Incest Survivors
Laurie Anne Pearlman and Karen W. Saakvitne

Psychological Trauma and the Adult Survivor:
Theory, Therapy, and Transformation
I. Lisa McCann and Laurie Anne Pearlman

A Norton Professional Book

Transforming the Pain
A Workbook on Vicarious Traumatization

Karen W. Saakvitne, Ph.D.
Laurie Anne Pearlman, Ph.D.

With the Staff of the
Traumatic Stress Institute/
Center for Adult & Adolescent Psychotherapy LLC

Daniel J. Abrahamson, Ph.D.
Amy Ehrlich Charney, Psy.D.
Sarah J. Gamble, Ph.D.
J. Mark Hall, Ph.D.
Sandra E. Hartdagen, Ph.D.
Anne C. Pratt, Ph.D.
Dena J. Rosenbloom, Ph.D.

W. W. Norton & Company · New York · London

For information about permission to reproduce selections from this
book, write to Permissions, W.W. Norton & Company, Inc.,
500 Fifth Avenue, New York, NY 10110.

Library of Congress Cataloging-in-Publication Data

Saakvitne, Karen W.
   Transforming the pain : a workbook on vicarious traumatization /
Karen W. Saakvitne, Laurie Anne Pearlman ; with the staff of the Trau-
matic Stress Institute/Center for Adult & Adolescent Psychotherapy,
Daniel J. Abrahamson . . . [et al].
         p.   cm.
   "A Norton Professional."
   Includes bibliographical references.
   ISBN 0-393-70233-2
   1. Post-traumatic stress disorder—Prevention. 2. Psychotherapists—
Job stress.   3. Emergency medical personnel—Job stress.   4. Psychic
trauma. 5. Burn out (Psychology)—Prevention. 6. Psychological debrief-
ing. I. Pearlman, Laurie A. II. Title.
RC552.P67S22 1996
616.85'21—dc20   96-21879
                                                                    CIP

W.W. Norton & Company, Inc., 500 Fifth Avenue,
New York, NY 10110
http://www.wwnorton.com
W.W. Norton & Company Ltd., 10 Coptic Street, London WC1A 1PU

9 0

To the thousands of workshop participants and trauma professionals who have shared with us their stories, their pain, their ways of replenishing and caring for themselves, and their commitment to the vital work we all do. Your words have touched and taught us.

Contents

About the Authors

Karen W. Saakvitne, Ph.D., (pronounced Saw-quit-knee) is the clinical director of TSI/CAAP and coauthor of *Trauma and the Therapist: Countertransference and Vicarious Traumatization in Psychotherapy with Incest Survivors*. Outside of work she likes to read, walk in New England woods, go to art museums, and turn her commute into self-care with recorded books.

Laurie Anne Pearlman, Ph.D., is the research director of TSI/CAAP and coauthor of *Psychological Trauma and the Adult Survivor: Theory, Therapy, and Transformation* and of *Trauma and the Therapist*. Her self-care program includes daily exercise, yoga, meditation, recorded books, reading novels, laughing, dancing, and spending as much time outdoors as possible.

Daniel J. Abrahamson, Ph.D., is the administrative director of TSI/CAAP. His political advocacy on behalf of psychological services compliments his clinical and administrative work and offsets vicarious traumatization. He enjoys travel and the laughter of his children.

Amy Ehrlich Charney, Psy.D., a licensed clinical psychologist, has been expanding her range of professional interests to include consultation and psychoeducational presentations. In her free time she nurtures her gardens, takes walks around reservoirs, and plays recreational soccer.

Sarah J. Gamble, Ph.D., is a licensed clinical psychologist. A former marathon runner, she combats work stress with outdoor activities, family time, and a part-time schedule.

J. Mark Hall, Ph.D., a licensed clinical psychologist, specializes in treatment of trauma survivors and in particular those with dissociative adaptations. He balances the stress of work with involvement in exercise, being a father, music, and being outdoors.

Sandra E. Hartdagen, Ph.D., a licensed clinical psychologist, works with a wide variety of adult clients and provides clinical supervision and consultation. Primary to ameliorating the negative impact of her clinical work is her commitment to her spiritual life through music, meditation, and yoga.

Anne C. Pratt, Ph.D., a licensed clinical and forensic psychologist, specializes in treatment and assessment of survivors of traumatic life events. To counter vicarious traumatization she enjoys singing, reading mysteries, and visiting historical sites with her family.

Dena J. Rosenbloom, Ph.D., a licensed clinical psychologist, works part-time and primarily sees adults and couples. She reserves her two extra days during the week to play with her son, hike, read, and discover interesting places to visit around New England.

Front row (from left): Laurie Anne Pearlman, Daniel J. Abrahamson, Karen W. Saakvitne; *back row:* Dena J. Rosenbloom, Sarah J. Gamble, J. Mark Hall, Anne C. Pratt, Sandra E. Hartdagen, Amy Ehrlich Charney.

Acknowledgments

So many people have contributed to the development of this workbook. The original inspiration came from participants in a 2-day vicarious traumatization workshop in Kenora, Ontario, who asked us to compile the exercises into a book. Throughout the years workshop participants have challenged us to elaborate our ideas and develop more strategies for addressing vicarious traumatization.

We want to thank Pamela Deiter, Ph.D., and Richard Nicastro, Ph.D., postdoctoral fellows at TSI/CAAP, for their contributions to this volume. Dr. Deiter provided a thoughtful reading and helpful editorial comments on early drafts. Dr. Nicastro provided the useful perspective of a newcomer to the concept of vicarious traumatization.

In addition, our administrative staff, Prudence Duzan, Molly Beaudoin, Susan Kupec, and Yvonne Corneau, and research assistants, Anna Maria Lucca and Robert Duzan, have provided invaluable support and contribute enormously to our work.

We are grateful to the many theoreticians and researchers investigating and writing about vicarious traumatization and related concepts, including Charles Figley, James Monroe, Christine Courtois, Judith Herman, Janet Yassen, Yael Danieli, Sarah Haley, Beth Hudnall Stamm, and others.

As always, we want to thank our editors, Susan Barrows Munro and Regina Dahlgren Ardini of W. W. Norton, for their enthusiasm for the project and pithy editorial advice.

Transforming the Pain
A Workbook on Vicarious Traumatization

Introduction

> I hadn't recognized under what a cloud I had allowed myself to slip. A ray of sunshine in a dark misty room! Thanks for the "inspiration."
>
> *—VT workshop participant, a crisis worker in a rural mental health agency*

Who Are We and Why Are We Writing this Workbook?

As trauma therapists, we know firsthand the personal cost of the work we do. As teachers and supervisors, we see students and colleagues struggle to make sense of powerful, often painful, feelings and changed beliefs. As researchers and scholars, we understand that it is impossible to hear and bear witness to trauma survivors' experiences and remain unchanged.

Vicarious traumatization (VT) refers to the cumulative transformative effect on the helper of working with survivors of traumatic life events. The truth is that we all are profoundly changed by the work we do with survivors of trauma. These changes are both positive and negative. We believe the rewards of trauma work balance the painful effects of vicarious traumatization. But we also believe all trauma workers must be aware of VT and its effects.

Having chosen these careers, we will never again be the same. Few of us entered the field fully understanding this truth. Few graduate programs focus on the experience of the therapist or the helper. Until recently, there was no construct to explain and make sense of a helper's natural responses to ongoing work with trauma survivors. Further, the mental health field often subscribes to the tenet—drawn in part from the medical model—that a professional doesn't "get involved" and that his or her feelings are signs of weakness, inadequacy, or poor boundaries. For therapists, these strictures are often reinforced by erroneous notions that countertransference is bad or reflects a therapist's unresolved issues (Freud, 1910).

The identification of the specific construct of vicarious traumatization by McCann and Pearlman (1990a) was a turning point for the field. Vicarious traumatization goes beyond the simple recognition that working with trauma survivors is hard and distressing to helpers. In that first paper, McCann and Pearlman described the pervasive effects of doing trauma therapy on the identity, world view, psychological needs, beliefs, and memory system of the therapist. Using constructivist self development theory (McCann & Pearlman, 1990b), they outline how and why our work changes us so profoundly. Their emphasis is on the unique interaction between the work experience and the self of the helper. Later elaborations of the concept of vicarious traumatization spell out the complex interactions among person, situation, and context examining multiple contributing factors (Pearlman & Saakvitne, 1995a, 1995b; Neumann & Gamble, 1995).*

With a detailed understanding of how one's work and self interact, one can identify and take the necessary steps to prevent and transform the negative effects of trauma work. The utility of the concept of vicarious traumatization is in its application; understanding the impact of our work and our own vulnerabilities allows us to prevent, ameliorate, and transform the negative impact of our work on our selves. Then we can enhance the positive impact of our work, including our sense of

---

* For further materials on vicarious traumatization, see references, annotated bibliography, and TSI/CAAP resources at the back of the workbook.

hope, our admiration for human resiliency, and our recognition of the difference one relationship can make in someone's healing and life.

This workbook will focus on application, describing strategies and techniques that we have found useful for helpers and therapists working with traumatized people. Our goal is to increase the positive effects of our work and minimize its negative or damaging impact on our lives and selves.

Who Can Benefit from this Workbook?

This workbook is written for any professional, paraprofessional, or volunteer who is working with clients who have been traumatized. If you serve or help those who have suffered trauma, you are at risk for vicarious traumatization. This book is relevant for mental health professionals and paraprofessionals, emergency personnel, medical personnel, crisis workers, community service workers, and educators. These people include but are not limited to:

> psychotherapists
> nurses
> social workers
> social service case workers
> Vista and Peace Corps volunteers
> hospice workers and bereavement counselors
> battered women's and homeless shelter staff
> sexual assault workers
> suicide hotline staff
> AIDS volunteers
> foster parents
> prison personnel
> veterans counselors
> military personnel

emergency medical technicians
fire fighters
police
criminal defense lawyers
prosecutors
judges
victim advocates

Vicarious traumatization is also relevant for trauma researchers, journalists, clergy, teachers, and others who work with victims and survivors; anyone who is repeatedly exposed to and empathically engaged with the stories of trauma survivors will find useful information and strategies in this workbook.

TSI/CAAP

The Traumatic Stress Institute/Center for Adult & Adolescent Psychotherapy_{LLC} is an independent mental health organization in South Windsor, Connecticut. Our clinical staff includes nine licensed clinical psychologists and two postdoctoral psychology fellows.* The organization has a dual mission: (1) to promote understanding and improve treatment of traumatic stress and (2) to promote psychology as a discipline and profession. The latter reflects our commitment to be a "Boulder model" organization, that is, one that integrates psychological research, clinical work, training, teaching, and community service. Our clinical work is informed by current research and our research is informed by clinical work—that is, by the words of our clients. Our overall goal is thus to provide psychologists with a supportive work

---

* In addition, our administrative staff of four and two part-time research assistants provide invaluable support and contribute enormously to our work.

setting in order to bring high quality psychological services to the public.

Because we recognize the relative dearth of professional training in trauma treatment and the concomitant high risk for damaging and unethical treatments with trauma survivors, we are committed to training and teaching in the field of traumatic stress. Within the organization this commitment is reflected in our two-year postdoctoral fellowship program, weekly individual supervision for all clinicians (one to two hours), and resources allocated to continuing education activities for all staff. Outside the organization this commitment is reflected in the seminars, talks, and workshops we present, and the books, workbooks, chapters, and papers we publish.

We see for ourselves, and for those we teach and supervise, the central role of vicarious traumatization in job satisfaction, mental and physical health, professional practice, and personal and professional development. We conclude that any training in trauma work MUST include education about vicarious traumatization and its management.

We strive to run our organization in a way that reflects this commitment to understand trauma treatment and address its effects on helpers. We integrate awareness of vicarious traumatization into our caseload structure, our internal supervision, our weekly case conference, our continuing education and vacation policies, and our biannual staff retreats. Based on our experiences, this workbook offers concrete suggestions to therapists and other mental health and crisis workers for addressing and transforming vicarious traumatization.

Our academic work reflects this commitment. We have written two books* since the inception of the organization in 1986, published numerous articles and book chapters, and conducted several research

---

* *Psychological Trauma and the Adult Survivor: Theory, Therapy, and Transformation* (McCann & Pearlman, 1990b) and *Trauma and the Therapist: Countertransference and Vicarious Traumatization in Psychotherapy with Incest Survivors* (Pearlman & Saakvitne, 1995a)

studies on vicarious traumatization and other topics in psychotherapy and trauma. Our workshops, in-service training, and professional education (including postdoctoral training) include attention to issues of vicarious traumatization and therapist self-care. In organizational consultations, as well as in group and individual supervisions, we integrate our understanding of vicarious traumatization into our feedback and recommendations. We have recently completed a two-part video presentation on vicarious traumatization, *Vicarious Traumatization I: The Pain of Empathy* and *Vicarious Traumatization II: Transforming the Pain.**

> It's been useful to me to change the teaching from religion "Do unto others as you would have them do unto you" into "Do unto yourself as you would do unto others."
>
> —*VT workshop participant, a graduate student in pastoral counseling doing an internship at a rape crisis center*

Using this Workbook

This workbook is organized in five chapters. The first summarizes the construct of vicarious traumatization. Here, we review the aspects of the self that are affected by vicarious traumatization and identify aspects of the work situation and the individual that place one at particular risk. Chapter 2 is about assessing and identifying vicarious traumatization. We describe tests and questionnaires that can be used by individuals or groups. The third chapter discusses general strategies

* For information on ordering any of the above materials, please call. For books and articles, call TSI/CAAP at (860) 644-2541. For the videos, call Cavalcade Productions at (800) 345-5530.

for addressing and transforming vicarious traumatization and identifies realms of impact and interventions. Chapter 4 is a collection of specific exercises and techniques for transforming vicarious traumatization within oneself, one's work, and one's personal life. The final chapter addresses the question of how one can maintain the commitment to continue addressing vicarious traumatization over time.

We hope you find this workbook helpful. Each reader will find certain parts uniquely meaningful or relevant. We encourage you to be an active reader, examining your own experience in light of the material and evaluating your own unique circumstances and resources. We hope you will gain a better understanding of the impact of your work on your self, and be able to identify specific and useful ways to improve your self-care and lessen the negative impact of your work.

Trauma workers make an invaluable contribution to our society. Whether you are new to your field or a long-time veteran, your energy, empathy, and creativity are resources that must be nurtured, safeguarded, and replenished. Just as you take seriously the impact of trauma in the lives of the individuals you serve, we hope this workbook will encourage you to extend the same level of commitment and compassion to yourself. Our aim is not only to limit the negative impact of trauma work, but also to enhance the growth-promoting and satisfying aspects of this work for you and your clients.

Please let us know what you find helpful and what other areas would be useful to include in future editions of this workbook.

Chapter 1
What Is Vicarious Traumatization?

> Finally! Somebody is talking about this important stuff.
> —*VT workshop participant, a therapist in private practice, a survivor of childhood sexual abuse*

Vicarious traumatization is the transformation of the therapist's or helper's inner experience as a result of empathic engagement with survivor clients and their trauma material. Simply put, when we open our hearts to hear someone's story of devastation or betrayal, our cherished beliefs are challenged and we are changed.

We view vicarious traumatization as an occupational hazard, an inescapable effect of trauma work. It is not something clients do to us; it is a human consequence of knowing, caring, and facing the reality of trauma.

A helper's vulnerability to vicarious traumatization is unavoidable if her work involves listening empathically to traumatized people with the goal of helping them. Taken together, her desire to help and her empathic engagement with traumatized clients create the conditions for vicarious traumatization.

Trauma workers strive to make a difference in the face of devastation. Our professional roles, personal and professional identities, and personal wishes to lessen the pain of others combine to create a powerful mandate to be effective. Yet the work is slow and often overwhelming; many helpers face initial failure and frustration when they hope for rapid success and transformation.

Empathy is a means of connection to an emotionally disenfranchised survivor. Often trauma workers are emotionally moved as they engage with their clients' past and present experiences. This empathic engagement makes the helper vulnerable to intense, sometimes overwhelming feelings and profoundly disrupted beliefs, the hallmarks of traumatic stress. Empathic pain together with disappointingly slow progress can translate into vicarious traumatization.

The specific impact of vicarious traumatization will be determined by the unique interaction between *the situation* (i.e., your work setting, type and number of clients and their traumas, nature of exposure to trauma, and the social, political, cultural contexts of both the original trauma[s] and the current work) and *the person of the helper* (i.e., your professional identity, resources, support, personal history, current life circumstances, coping style).

Trauma always involves loss; after a trauma nothing is ever again the same. This profound loss of the familiar is another hallmark of trauma. As trauma workers, we confront this reality every day. We then must also face our own vulnerability to such loss, both in our own lives and in the lives of those we love. Trauma work assaults our self-protective beliefs about safety, control, predictability, and protection.

> One 27-year-old woman reflected on changes in her beliefs about safety after her first year of counseling adult sexual assault survivors. "I used to feel pretty safe and self-confident in the world. I never paid such attention to locks and security and protection as I do now. I won't live in a first-floor apartment, I won't walk alone at night, I have double locks on my doors and an alarm system, and I took a model mugging class—all since I started working as a counselor at the rape crisis center."

> A 45-year-old EMT explained, "My teenage kids think I am an ogre because I am so strict with them about curfews and

driving. I don't ever let them drive with teenage drivers or let the older one drive without me or his mother in the car. I know they think this is excessive, but they haven't seen the accidents I've seen. I guess I wish that by making rules I can protect them from the horrors I've seen."

How to Recognize Vicarious Traumatization

Constructivist Self Development Theory

In order to understand what vicarious traumatization looks like, one needs to understand how trauma changes a person. Because the concept of vicarious traumatization is based in constructivist self development theory (CSDT), it is helpful to know the basic outline of that theory. CSDT describes the aspects of the self that are affected by traumatic events. Vicarious traumatization will affect helpers in the same ways, although to a lesser degree. Understanding which aspects of self are vulnerable to disruption helps one identify and then transform one's particular experiences of vicarious traumatization.

CSDT says that traumatic events impact a person in the context of her developing self. In the face of trauma, each person will adapt and cope given her current context(s) and early experiences: interpersonal, intrapsychic, familial, cultural, and social. Within these contexts, the theory outlines the impact of trauma on the self (McCann & Pearlman, 1990b; Pearlman & Saakvitne, 1995a).

CSDT emphasizes adaptation and the active construction of meaning. This approach views "symptoms" as adaptations to events. Adaptations are based on the context in which an event occurs and its meaning to the individual. Our theory assumes that "irrational" or distorted beliefs reflect an attempt to protect oneself and one's meaning system from the harm that the trauma threatens. This theory differs, then, from traditional models that focus on pathology, symptoms, diagnoses, and specific events.

For example, the intense shame commonly experienced by adult survivors of childhood abuse is seen as a result of constructions of meaning in childhood that served to protect the child's image of his or her parents. "They are right and good, so I must deserve this pain because I am unworthy and bad." The corollary that the child is responsible for his or her abuse protects the parents and reinforces the child's wish-based belief in her power and control. These beliefs help the child to deny her own powerlessness (and thus not feel so terrified and helpless).

In adulthood, this shame and guilt can be reflected in cycles of self-abuse and self-defeating behaviors. If, as helpers, we try to stop these behaviors *without* understanding the beliefs they serve to protect, we will fail. Beliefs and behaviors can change only as the survivor gains relief from her internal conflicts and anxiety and has an opportunity to address her rage and grief. Yet without a framework to understand the meaning of symptoms, a helper's efforts are often unsuccessful; when we are repeatedly unsuccessful, our frustration, discouragement, and despair put us and our work at risk.

CSDT Components of Self
Frame of Reference
Self Capacities
Ego Resources
Psychological Needs and Cognitive Schemas
Memory and Perception

Frame of Reference

The self includes frame of reference: the underlying sense of identity, world view, and spirituality that informs the individual's perception of herself, her world, her relationships and her experiences. Combined, these beliefs create the lens through which she views the world and interprets her experiences.

Frame of Reference

Identity

World view

Spirituality

Self Capacities

An individual's experience of self is strongly shaped by her capacities for inner balance, specifically capacities (a) to manage strong feelings, (b) to feel entitled to be alive and deserving of love, and (c) to hold onto an inner awareness of caring others. These self capacities set the stage for how someone understands and integrates significant events in her life and her feelings about them. They are reflected in an individual's abilities to self-soothe and maintain a sense of inner equilibrium.

Self Capacities

Affect tolerance

Sense of self as viable

Inner connection with others

Ego Resources

The self also includes the individual's abilities to negotiate interpersonal situations and to make good decisions. In CSDT, we call these ego resources. They include skills in self-awareness (skills helpful in therapy), for example, insight, taking the perspective of another (including empathy and a sense of humor), using willpower and initiative, and striving for personal growth. Ego resources also include skills important in interpersonal relationships, for example, being able to foresee consequences, make self-protective judgments, and establish healthy boundaries between oneself and others.

At any given time, a person's self capacities and ego resources will be more or less available depending on their development and reinforcement in childhood and on her current level of arousal or distress.

Ego Resources

Self-awareness skills

Interpersonal and self-protective skills

Psychological Needs and Cognitive Schemas

The self includes basic psychological needs and one's beliefs about those needs. CSDT defines five major needs that are sensitive to traumatic events: safety, esteem, trust (or dependence), control, and intimacy. These are reflected in beliefs (schemas) about oneself (e.g., self-trust, self-esteem) and others (e.g., trust in others, esteem for others).

Psychological Needs and Cognitive Schemas

Safety

Esteem

Trust

Control

Intimacy

Memory and Perception

Finally, CSDT recognizes that memory and perception are complex and multimodal. Any experience is processed and recalled through several modalities, including the cognitive (narrative), visual, affective (emotional), somatic and sensory, and interpersonal (behavioral). Thus, a complete (nonfragmented) memory is encoded along all of these dimensions, which are integrated and interconnected. Traumatic memories often involve the dissociation or disconnection of different aspects of the experience. The resulting memory is fragmented. For example, the narrative may be recalled without the feelings or images, or the feeling (e.g., panic or terror) or an image (e.g., flashback) without a narrative context.

Memory and Perception

Narrative, sequential

Visual, images

Affective

Sensory, somatic

Interpersonal, behavioral

The table on the following two pages summarizes CSDT.

Signs of Vicarious Traumatization

Signs of vicarious traumatization will be evident in the same areas of the self for helpers as for survivors: frame of reference, self capacities, ego resources, psychological needs and cognitive schemas, and perception and memory.

Thus a trauma worker may find herself feeling disconnected from her sense of identity.

>*"I am a person who wants to help others. Why am I constantly enraged with my clients?"*

>*"Why do I feel nothing when yet another client tells me about her sexual abuse? I used to be such a caring person."*

A trauma worker's fundamental beliefs about the world often change.

>*"I used to believe the world was basically fair and that people were basically good. Now I think fate is fickle and I don't trust anyone."*

>*"I used to think life was predictable; now I know anything can happen at any time."*

Constructivist Self Development Theory
Aspects of the Self Impacted by Psychological Trauma

Frame of Reference

Framework of beliefs through which the individual interprets experience

- Identity: inner experience of self and self in the world, includes customary feeling states
- World view: life philosophy, general attitudes and beliefs about others and the world; values and moral principles; causality
- Spirituality: meaning, hope, faith; connection with something beyond oneself, awareness of all aspects of life including the non-material

Self Capacities

Abilities that enable the individual to maintain a sense of self as consistent and coherent across time and situations; intrapersonal

- Ability to experience, tolerate, and integrate strong affect
- Ability to maintain a sense of self as viable, benign, and positive, deserving of life and love
- Ability to maintain an inner sense of connection with others

Ego Resources

Abilities that enable the individual to meet psychological needs and to relate to others; interpersonal

- Self-awareness skills
  Intelligence
  Ability to be introspective
  Willpower and initiative
  Ability to strive for personal growth
  Awareness of psychological needs
  Ability to take perspective
- Interpersonal and self-protective skills
  Ability to foresee consequences
  Ability to establish mature relations with others
  Ability to establish interpersonal boundaries
  Ability to make self-protective judgments

***Constructivist Self Development Theory,* continued**

Psychological Needs and Cognitive Schemas

- Safety

    Self: to feel reasonably invulnerable to harm inflicted by one-self or others

    Other: to feel that valued others are reasonably invulnerable to harm inflicted by oneself or others

- Esteem

    Self: to feel valued by oneself and others

    Other: to value others

- Trust/dependency

    Self: to have confidence in one's own judgment and ability to meet one's needs

    Other: to have confidence in others to meet one's needs

- Control

    Self: to feel able to manage one's feelings and behaviors in interpersonal situations

    Other: to feel able to manage or exert control over others in interpersonal situations

- Intimacy

    Self: to feel connected to oneself

    Other: to feel connected to others

Memory and Perception

- Verbal: the narrative of what happened before, during, and after the trauma

- Imagery: the mental pictures of the traumatic events

- Affect: the emotions related to the trauma

- Somatic: the bodily experiences that represent the traumatic events

- Interpersonal: the relational patterns and behaviors that reflect the abusive traumatic relationship(s)

One's sense of spirituality may change or simply fade.

> *"I considered myself a deeply spiritual person, but I don't know where that sense of connection to the universe has gone."*
>
> *"I feel alone—isolated and cut off in an existential sense these days."*
>
> *"I used to enjoy and get great comfort from my church. But now I have several clients who were violated by religious leaders and I think of them when I go to church. It's a real loss."*

Trauma professionals often find they feel less grounded and can't maintain a sense of inner balance. Their feelings may seem overwhelming; they have crying jags or eruptions of anger. They become intolerant or frustrated, unbearably anxious or chronically unable to experience pleasure. Some shut down emotionally and feel numb, hard, distant, or depersonalized. Trauma workers can lose touch with their inner connection to important people and become unable to hold their loved ones in their minds or to know they are being thought of lovingly.

These disruptions create disconnection and can leave one in existential despair and aloneness. At this point some individuals cannot feel they are loved or deserve to be loved; others may question their right to be alive or to be happy. This loss of grounding is terrifying and is often expressed by the clients with whom we work. Clearly a helper is limited in her ability to hold onto faith and hope for her clients when she herself feels despair or self-loathing. Although these feelings may be transient, they can be deeply unsettling.*

---

* When pervasive or unchanging, severe, or experienced as a cluster, these symptoms may, of course, also suggest depression, anxiety, or other affective or stress disorders that indicate the need for consultation and possible treatment. Sometimes the constellation of distressing symptoms reflects a degree of impairment that interferes with professional functioning. A consultation can help one assess when a vacation, increased supervision, personal psychotherapy, or a leave of absence seem indicated.

A child therapist working in a community agency with many clients who had been sexually abused wrote, "After a time, I just cried at everything. I felt as though I had no skin. I cried at the radio, the television, commercials, the newspaper, and anything I read. I'd pass kids at a playground and cry. I felt out of control. I was giving so much at work, I didn't have anything left to manage my own grief about the cruelty to children in our society."

When a helper's ego resources are compromised, she is less likely to make decisions that are in her own best interest, and may make professional errors in boundaries, judgment, or strategy. She may be less self-reflective and therefore unable to sort out her own feelings and responses from those of her clients. She may fail to set limits and may overextend herself, leading to inevitable failure, resentment, and exhaustion. A psychotherapist will be less able to notice and then analyze and use her own countertransference, thus leaving the therapy vulnerable to countertransference enactments.

A therapist at a community clinic realized, "I stopped paying attention to what I could *do and just focused on what I felt I* must *do to make up to my clients for the horrible things they had suffered."*

A therapist in a feminist group practice shared, "At any given moment, I would decide I could do one more session, or give up one more hour, because after all I had such a good life and they had such awful lives. Who was I to deserve all this good luck? I hadn't been brutalized as a child."

Inevitably helpers notice changes in their beliefs within basic need areas. Anyone working with trauma survivors has some change in beliefs about safety—one's own and that of loved ones.

A school psychologist working with kids who are victims of abuse realized, "I can't let my kids play outside of the yard. I don't feel they're safe with anyone else—even my husband sometimes."

A guard at a prison confessed, "I have triple locks on all my doors now. I never used to be this way."

Many therapists working with survivors or perpetrators of childhood abuse struggle to feel comfortable with their own childcare decisions.

One new mother, a clinician who worked with adult survivors of childhood sexual abuse, explained, "Interviewing potential baby-sitters was a nightmare. I was afraid I couldn't trust my judgment. I kept thinking, 'Some people who perpetrate the most sadistic abuse look totally fine on the surface.'"

Changes in self-trust and trust in others are also common as one is exposed to reports of dangers that couldn't be prevented and to the potential for betrayal by seemingly trustworthy people (e.g., the upstanding community member who abuses his children behind closed doors). Further, working with chronically suicidal clients challenges our trust in ourselves, our decisions, and our assessments and reminds us of the limits of our ability to judge and predict others' behaviors.

One senior male clinician reported, "I found myself doubting my colleagues. Whenever I heard a client complain about another therapist, I immediately assumed the worst, that the therapist was doing something terrible and unethical. I had lost my faith in humanity, in my gender, and in the profession. I mistrusted all male therapists, and instead of listening to the client's material, I acted as judge and jury."

Some of us react to the loss of control and helplessness inherent in trauma by trying to maintain control over as many aspects of our lives as possible.

> *One child protective services caseworker stated, "I thought if I could just keep track of everything then nothing bad could happen to me or to my family. I know better, but I was compelled to be in control at all times. I would get furious at anyone who got in the way or took over for me."*

Others give up trying to control any aspect of their lives as their exposure to clients' traumatic experiences bring them face to face with the limits of control.

> *"It was as though if I gave into my powerlessness, then I was less helpless. It doesn't really make sense, but it felt as though it did. If I didn't try, then I wouldn't have failed to protect myself."*

> *One therapist sought consultation because she felt beleaguered by managed care reviews for her clients, and had started to miss deadlines and not appeal decisions with which she disagreed. After examining her motives, she realized, "I accepted the message that I was powerless. I started to feel like all my clients did as kids, that no matter what I or they did, it would make no difference. I ran out of hope and the energy to fight back, but especially I lost perspective. I felt like a helpless child—as were many of my clients—and then I just gave up because I 'knew' I'd lose—as many of them did."*

Vicarious traumatization has a profound effect on relationships with others. In addition to changes in safety, trust, and control schemas, a trauma worker's beliefs about intimacy with others and

with himself may alter. He may be unable to be open in intimate relationships because of his increased or decreased access to his emotions.
If his intimates are not also trauma workers he may feel increasingly
isolated both by the constraints of confidentiality and by others' inabil-
ity to understand the stresses of trauma work. Many individuals who
work with survivors of sexual trauma struggle with intrusive imagery
that disturbs their sexual relationships. Others experience guilt and
intrusive thoughts about their clients' traumas that prevent them from
experiencing unconflicted desire and pleasure. This problem, while not
uncommon, is rarely addressed (Maltz, 1992).

> *A 35-year-old lesbian who worked as a victim advocate in a
> district attorney's office lamented, "I can't make love with my
> partner now without being tormented by these awful images or
> hearing the words of my clients' perpetrators. Then I lose all
> interest in being sexual, and my partner gets hurt and frustrated.
> It's hard to explain to her, because of course I have to keep my
> client's confidentiality—and I wouldn't want to burden her with
> these images anyway."*

Finally, a trauma worker may experience significant changes in
esteem for herself or others.

> *A grassroots organizer and shelter volunteer confessed, "I
> found I was subtly contemptuous of anyone who didn't work in
> the field of victims' rights, as though no other work were worth-
> while."*

> *A member of a community program that provides support
> for at-risk families explained, "I realized that the people we
> were working with had so many problems and had experienced
> such horrific life experiences that I felt guilty for my relatively
> easy life. I got more and more critical of myself when I was*

down or tired. I would berate myself, saying I had no right and no reason to feel bad because my life was comparatively so much better than their lives."

Other important signs of vicarious traumatization are intrusive imagery (visual, auditory, olfactory, sensory), and other symptoms that parallel PTSD symptomatology (nightmares, avoidance of reminders of traumatic events, numbing, social withdrawal, emotional flooding).

A judge who presided over several child abuse trials realized he felt "triggered" when at his granddaughter's playground he saw a man pushing a little girl on the swing. "I couldn't get it out of my head that he was untrustworthy and would harm her later. I had been so immersed in these trials, I had lost all perspective. I kept having intrusive imagery from the photographs shown at the trial. I had to look away to get them out of my head."

A social worker reported, "My partner and I were house hunting and looked at several older homes. I realized I could not go with her into the basements because I was flooded with pictures of what had happened to my clients in basements One client in particular had described the musty smell she associated with abuse, and I was aware of that smell in the basements."

Now I understand why I've been having nightmares all the time through this trial.

—*Participant in a VT workshop for victim advocates in the courts*

The imagery that plagues an individual will often reflect the psychological needs that are most important to him or her. Thus when we are

Vicarious Traumatization

Definition

A transformation of the helper's inner experience, resulting from empathic engagement with clients' trauma material.

Signs and Symptoms

General changes

- No time or energy for oneself
- Disconnection from loved ones
- Social withdrawal
- Increased sensitivity to violence
- Cynicism
- Generalized despair and hopelessness
- Nightmares

Specific changes

- Disrupted frame of reference
- Changes in identity, world view, spirituality
- Diminished self capacities
- Impaired ego resources
- Disrupted psychological needs and cognitive schemas
- Alterations in sensory experiences (intrusive imagery, dissociation, depersonalization)

Contributing Factors

The situation

- Nature of the work
- Nature of the clientele
- Cumulative exposure to trauma material
- Organizational context
- Social and cultural context

The individual

- Personal history
- Personality and defensive style
- Coping style
- Current life context
- Training and professional history
- Supervision
- Personal therapy

tormented by a particular story, it usually echoes something specific about our own needs and beliefs that has been challenged or activated, as well as something about our relationship with the client and the client's unique history and story. When the same kinds of stories or experiences trouble us across clients, it is a clue that these images mirror some important need or belief of ours. Then the effect of a particular client's troubling story merges with the impact of other stories and interactions with other trauma clients, creating a cumulative effect.

Vicarious traumatization is a process, not an event. It includes our strong feelings and our defenses against those feelings. Thus vicarious traumatization is our strong reactions of grief, rage, and outrage, which grow as we repeatedly hear about and see people's pain and loss and are forced to recognize human potential for cruelty and indifference, *and* it is our numbing, our protective shell, and our wish not to know, which follow those reactions. These two alternating states of numbness and overwhelming feelings parallel the experience of PTSD.

What Contributes to Vicarious Traumatization?

I see a lot of institutionalized VT in women's shelters and rape crisis centers. Women who work in women's organizations are often survivors, and they are retraumatized by administrative and funding structures in addition to the stress of their work.

—VT workshop participant, an executive director of an urban rape crisis center

Aspects of the Work

The nature of our work contributes to vicarious traumatization. Some of us have only brief crisis contact with trauma survivors, at the time when they are most distressed. In that context we expect ourselves (and they and others expect us) to make a significant difference. At the same time, since the survivor's experience is often one of extreme powerlessness, we may identify with the enormity of the impact of trauma and feel overwhelmed. Further, in this brief contact we are often exposed to either the details of someone's traumatic experiences or the details of the traumatic effects. We often get no feedback about how our helping efforts did or did not make a difference. We connect, we care, and then our clients are gone; we do not know the rest of their healing process.

Professionals who work with survivors for longer periods of time see more of the recovery and healing process, but they also see how slow and painful this journey can be. Workers are often drawn into reenactments and must sort out the complicated projective processes that characterize relationships with people who have been repeatedly hurt by others.

Short-term crisis work or more extended work: Is one better than the other for the helper? That depends on the individual's interpersonal and coping styles. You need to know yourself in order to assess which challenges best fit your interpersonal and coping styles. If you do better being active and working on problem-solving, you may prefer short-term work. If you prefer to feel deeply with someone and have time to go through a process together, you may be more comfortable in longer-term work.

One's work setting has a profound effect on his or her vulnerability to vicarious traumatization. Vicarious traumatization is a reality, yet many agencies that deal with traumatized clients operate out of misguided beliefs that feelings are unprofessional and have no place in the workplace. This shortsighted and unrealistic view increases the risk of vicarious traumatization for professionals within the organization and ultimately for the organization as a whole. It endangers clients and treaters, and it hurts organizations, through employee attrition, absenteeism, and professional misconduct.

The results can be disastrous when organizations

- provide no respite for the staff (e.g., shared coverage, adequate time off)
- require staff to have unrealistically high caseloads
- fail to provide enough qualified supervision
- deny the severity and pervasiveness of clients' traumatic experiences and their aftereffects
- fail to work with staff to identify and address signs of vicarious traumatization
- do not provide opportunities for continuing education
- do not provide sufficient vacation time
- do not support personal psychotherapy for clinicians (e.g., health insurance, acknowledgment of the value and importance of personal therapy for all clinicians)

Service organizations must recognize that addressing vicarious traumatization is part of a reasonable standard of practice for any profession that entails direct service to traumatized clients. The cost of not doing so is immeasurable. At a time when much of our work is under scrutiny from several angles, we cannot fail to protect our professions by maintaining high standards of ethics, professionalism, and effective care. Supporting trauma workers also benefits organizations financially as it decreases absenteeism, employee turnover, and unethical practices.

Other factors that contribute to vicarious traumatization are outlined below.

Our Clients

- Their multiple problems and limited resources
- The horror of their abusive histories

- The poignancy and intensity of their suffering
- The crisis of a recent traumatic experience
- The difficulty of their interpersonal style, often developed in response to untrustworthy or exploitative contexts
- Their idealized or intense negative expectations of the helper
- Current dangers they may be facing (safety concerns)
- The terror and shame that keep them paralyzed
- Helplessness and vulnerability of child clients
- Their self destructive behaviors, self-hatred, despair, and chronic suicidal wishes

Ourselves, the Helpers

- Unrealistic expectations for oneself as a professional
- A personal history of trauma that may be reawakened by client material and may make one particularly sensitive to certain transferences or expectations from clients
- Unfounded beliefs about the value of stoicism or nonresponsiveness that leave the professional feeling ashamed and silenced about her feelings
- Personal coping strategies that do not help or carry heavy costs (e.g., addictions, numbness, isolation)
- Current stressful personal life circumstances
- Working in areas in which a helper has insufficient training or inadequate theoretical understanding of the issues
- Reluctance or barriers to using supervision and consultation, seeking continuing education, or taking vacations
- Being new to the field of trauma work (see Neumann & Gamble, 1995)

Our Context

- A social context that denies or underrates trauma and its aftereffects
- A political context that underfunds psychological treatment for trauma
- A cultural context that blames the victim and glorifies violence and victimization as entertainment
- An organizational context that treats clients disrespectfully
- An organizational context that fails to provide staff the resources necessary to do the work they believe they can do on behalf of their clients

> The workshop has given me a language and a way of thinking about how and why some employees in organizations react the way they do and how organizations aggravate their negativity, e.g., guards in jails being so abusive to one another, child welfare workers' interpersonal conflicts.
>
> —*VT workshop participant, an administrator for a state EAP*

Vicarious Traumatization and Psychotherapy*

In psychotherapy, trauma material includes graphic descriptions of violent events, exposure to the realities of people's cruelty to one another, and involvement in trauma-related reenactments, either as a participant or as a bystander. It includes being a helpless witness to past

---

* For more detailed discussion of the therapist's experience of countertransference and vicarious traumatization in psychotherapy with adult survivors of childhood abuse, see Pearlman and Saakvitne (1995a).

events and current reenactments. Our clients' vivid descriptions of their brutal victimizations often stay with us and intrude as unbidden and profoundly disturbing images or sensations.

As therapists, our capacity for empathy is an essential gift and tool, yet our empathy is also a source of our vulnerability to vicarious traumatization. Therapy with survivors of childhood abuse confronts us with the harsh, painful reality of cruelty, selfishness, and evil actions.

Many trauma survivors remember their painful experiences and abusive relationships through reliving them in interpersonal (and intrapersonal) reenactments. Exposure to and participation in these reenactments is an additional, independent contributor to vicarious traumatization. This can take the form of witnessing a client's repeated self-destructive behaviors and being unable to protect him or oneself from the trauma. These reenactments often include replaying roles of victim, perpetrator, helpless or nonprotective bystander, rescuer, or protected or unprotected sibling (Miller, 1994; Davies & Frawley, 1994). When these reenactments occur outside the therapy, a therapist can feel like a helpless witness. When they occur within the therapeutic relationship, the therapist struggles with difficult countertransference responses and identity conflicts. Cumulatively, a therapist comes to feel battered, helpless, and often guilty and confused when trying to sort out these complex conscious and unconscious events in multiple therapies with trauma survivors.

The Countertransference-Vicarious Traumatization Cycle

While vicarious traumatization and countertransference are distinct constructs and experiences, *they affect one another.* Countertransference is present in all therapies, but is specific to a given client and the particular therapist-client dyad. The effects of vicarious traumatization are the result of an accumulation of experiences across therapies *and* are felt beyond a particular therapy relationship, that is, in other therapy relationships and in the therapist's personal and professional life. Vicarious traumatization is permanently transformative, while countertransference is temporally and temporarily linked to a particular period, event, or issue in the therapy or in the therapist's inner or external life as it interacts with the therapy.

A therapist reported in supervision that in a recent session with a survivor client who was depressed, angry, and self-hating, he found himself agreeing with her despair and unable to reassure her that things would get better. He was horrified to realize he thought she might be right when she said she would be better off dead. He felt deeply ashamed of his loss of hope for the therapy process and wondered if he was "burned out" or simply a terrible person. His supervisor encouraged him to think aloud about what he was feeling during the session about the client and about the work.

After exploration, he identified two major themes. One, this particular client was not only depressed but also angry. Yet she did not directly speak her anger, but expressed it in relentless attacks on his optimism and hope. His countertransference response was to agree with her despair out of anger, thus paralleling her passive aggression and conflict avoidance. Two, he had a particularly difficult group of clients in general and on that day in particular and was feeling painfully aware of the extent of abusive childhood experiences among his clients and the parallel degree of mistrust, despair, shame, and self-loathing experienced by so many of them. He felt saddened and exhausted by his realization of the pervasive effects of childhood abuse and neglect. His vicarious traumatization was evident in his flagging sense of hope, optimism, and energy.

Vicarious traumatization affects countertransference. Vicarious traumatization changes the self of the therapist, which is the context for all countertransference responses. Thus vicarious traumatization invariably shapes countertransference. As a therapist experiences greater vicarious traumatization, his countertransference responses can become stronger and/or less available to conscious awareness. This situation can lead to clinical error and therapeutic impasse and can result in even more vicarious traumatization, as the therapist's identity and esteem are further challenged and the rewards of his work decrease.

Countertransference affects vicarious traumatization because it influences our expectations for ourselves and our clients. For example, when in a maternal protective countertransference, the therapist is more vulnerable to shame when a client is slow to improve and intense guilt when a client gets worse or hurts herself. When countertransference anger leads us to be unempathic to a client, we can rapidly lose hope in the work and the profession in a scramble to protect our self-esteem.

Damage to Hope

> Vicarious traumatization also carries a social cost. . . .
> Unaddressed vicarious traumatization, manifest in cynicism and despair, results in a loss to society of hope and the positive actions it fuels. This loss can be experienced by our clients, as we at times join them in their despair; by our friends and families, as we no longer interject optimism, joy, and love into our shared pursuits; and in the larger systems in which we were once active as change agents, and which we may now leave, or withdraw from emotionally in a state of disillusionment and resignation. (Pearlman & Saakvitne, 1995a, p. 33)

Perhaps the most insidious impact of vicarious traumatization over time is its assault on our hope and idealism. Many of us who work with victims entered our fields with the wish to be helpful and the belief that we could make a difference. We may have had naive expectations about the rapidity of change and were probably unprepared for the toll this work takes. Yet our hope and optimism are essential gifts we bring to our work.

However, both as a direct result of vicarious traumatization and in defense against it, it is all too easy to give into cynicism and pessimism. "If you never hope, then you can't be disappointed," as many of our clients remind us. If you give in to despair then you don't have to keep trying and struggling. An enormous part of what we offer our clients is our belief in healing and change. Victor Frankl (1959), whose theory grew out of his experiences and observations in Nazi concentration camps, asserts that hope is essential in psychotherapy. We concur. Those who work with victims of trauma must continue to believe in new possibilities for these clients. While the past will influence the present and future, it does not have to dictate them.

Those who work with survivors of trauma cannot afford to give up hope. This is not to say that individuals will not or should not choose to leave the field or enter a different kind of work. For some trauma workers, the cost of vicarious traumatization is too high. For some, the compromises are too great. For some, the benefits of a professional change are important for their own happiness and personal relationships. Such decisions need not reflect cynicism or loss of faith. Each of us must find the place where our gifts are most needed and appreciated and where we find replenishment in our giving.

Addressing vicarious traumatization is an ethical imperative. We have an obligation to our clients—as well as to ourselves, our colleagues, and our loved ones—not to be damaged by the work we do. Specifically, many traumatized clients live with the fear that they will harm others through their needs or feelings; we are responsible to make sure they do not harm us. It is our responsibility to take care of ourselves and to set the limits on our availability and role that allow us to do our work and not be depleted or harmed.

> Validating experience—wish it were taught in social work schools.
> —*VT workshop participant, a recent MSW working in an AIDS treatment program*

Chapter 2
Assessing Vicarious Traumatization

I identified my VT symptoms and then the shame was removed for me about having VT. And I got some ways to address it.

—*VT workshop participant, a police officer who works on a child abuse prevention team*

It is easier to protect yourself from vicarious traumatization if you know your vulnerabilities. This chapter contains several worksheets to help you identify your own signs of vicarious traumatization. These worksheets can be done individually, in collaboration with a colleague, in supervision, or in small peer groups. We hope these tools will be jumping-off points for developing a group to address vicarious traumatization (see chapter 3), for making organizational changes (see chapter 5), and for making important personal changes (see chapters 3 and 4).

Some of the questions may be difficult or require time to answer. It may be helpful to discuss them with a colleague, consultant, or therapist. Consulting about vicarious traumatization and other emotional distress is part of self-care and health. (We emphasize this point because so many helpers are surprisingly resistant to seeking help for themselves.)

Personal Assessment Tools

Three worksheets for personal assessment of vicarious traumatization follow. The first worksheet draws upon the discussion in the prior chapter of factors that contribute to and increase vicarious traumatization. The second invites attention to your current emotional experience. The third uses the CSDT model of self to assess what aspects of yourself may show evidence of vicarious traumatization. Answers to the questions they pose will provide important information for next steps, discussed in the next three chapters.

Contributing Factors

The Nature of the Work

How much choice and control do I have over my work?

Is my work short-term, crisis, or long-term?

Am I doing the kind of work
  a. I like?

  b. for which I feel well-suited?

  c. at which I feel competent and talented?

Does this work match my values and beliefs?

The Nature of the Clientele

With what populations do I work?

How many clients do I see?
  each day?

  each week?

Is there balance and variety in my caseload and work?

Transforming the Pain: A Workbook on Vicarious Traumatization
Saakvitne, Pearlman. & Staff of TSI/CAAP (Norton. 1996)

Are there certain clients with whom I especially enjoy working? Why?

With which clients do I struggle the most? Why?

Other client-related factors?

The Nature of the Workplace

Do I have enough organizational support?

Do I have collegial support (within my organization, within my profession, among collateral providers)?

Am I getting enough helpful supervision?

Other workplace factors?

The Nature of the Helper: Self Assessment

Is my training appropriate for my work?

What are my current life stressors and supports?

Transforming the Pain: A Workbook on Vicarious Traumatization
Saakvitne, Pearlman, & Staff of TSI/CAAP (Norton, 1996)

What is my relevant life history?

What are my familiar coping strategies?

What are my emotional style and vulnerabilities?

How is the fit between myself and my work?

Do I enjoy my work?

Other personal factors?

The Nature of the Social/Cultural Context

How am I impacted by social obstacles to the work (e.g., funding cuts to mental health, managed care, delayed recall controversy)?

How does the community respond to the type of work I (and my organization) am doing?

How does the community view the population I serve?

Transforming the Pain: A Workbook on Vicarious Traumatization
Saakvitne, Pearlman, & Staff of TSI/CAAP (Norton, 1996)

Distress Level

> Read each paragraph separately and simply think about the questions each poses. Notice what comes to mind and be open to the information about yourself.

At the end of each day and at the end of your work week, how would you rate your emotional stress level? What do you notice in your body, your mind, and your feelings as you leave the office? How do you feel as you commute to work? as you commute home? when you arrive home? after an hour home? as you fall asleep? Do you dream about your work? If so, what are the themes and imagery in these dreams?

Do you notice some days are more difficult or that some seem easier? Is there a pattern you can detect? Are there certain clients or types of clients with whom it feels more stressful to be in a relationship? Do you understand why they are more difficult for you? Has that always been true? Are there certain tasks or responsibilities that are particularly stressful for you? Do you know why? How does your daily scheduling affect your state of mind?

How do you use your leisure time? What is relaxing for you? How long does it take to relax on a weekend? Are you using drugs, food, alcohol, gambling, or shopping to soothe yourself? Do you need drugs or alcohol to induce or maintain sleep? Do you or people close to you notice consistent patterns of tension, emotionality or reactivity, withdrawal, depression, fatigue, or cynicism?

Remember to include external as well as internal information. What changes in your behaviors have you noticed? What do you do that you did not used to do? What do you no longer do that was once familiar behavior? What changes in your body and health do you notice? Has your relationship with your body changed—in exercise, diet, sexuality, relaxation, or posture? What changes do you see in your relationships with others—with colleagues, friends, lovers, partners, children, other family members, neighbors, strangers, or helpers? What about your relationship with yourself? What has changed or failed to change? What do you appreciate more as a result of this work?

Transforming the Pain: A Workbook on Vicarious Traumatization
Saakvitne, Pearlman, & Staff of TSI/CAAP (Norton, 1996)

Signs of VT

> As a result of your work with trauma victims, survivors, or perpetrators, what *changes* have you noticed in the following areas of your life and beliefs?

Frame of Reference

My identity and beliefs about myself: Who am I?

My view of and beliefs about the world: How do I see it?

My spirituality (sense of connectedness and meaning, and faith): How has it changed?

My work motivation: Are my reasons for doing this work different from when I started it?

Self Capacities: My Inner Sense of Balance

How am I managing strong feelings?

Can I keep loved ones in my mind and know they care about me?

Do I feel worthwhile, deserving, and lovable?

Transforming the Pain: A Workbook on Vicarious Traumatization
Saakvitne, Pearlman, & Staff of TSI/CAAP (Norton, 1996)

Ego Resources: Using My Resources on My Own Behalf

Am I using my resources to make good decisions in personal and professional relationships (self-protective judgment, boundaries)?

Am I using my resources to know myself better (introspection) and to keep growing (insight, striving for personal growth)?

Basic Psychological Needs and My Beliefs about Them

a. *Safety* for myself and those I love

Do I feel reasonably safe?

Do I believe my loved ones are safe?

b. *Esteem* for myself and other people

Am I proud of who I am?

Do I believe others deserve respect?

c. *Trust* in myself and other people

Do I believe I can trust my own judgment?

Do I believe I can trust or depend on others?

d. *Control* in my life and over others

Do I believe I have control over my life?

Do I believe I can influence others' behavior?

Transforming the Pain: A Workbook on Vicarious Traumatization
Saakvitne, Pearlman, & Staff of TSI/CAAP (Norton, 1996)

e. *Intimacy* and closeness with myself and others

Do I believe I am good company for myself?

Do I believe I can be close to others?

Changes in Sensory Experiences: Intrusive Imagery, Sensations

Do I experience more nightmares?

Do I have intrusive thoughts about my own or others' safety?

Do I experience intrusive images or sensory experiences?

Am I reactive to triggers connected to my clients' experiences?

Has my contentment with or response to my sexuality changed?

a. How have my sexual behaviors changed?

b. Do I experience intrusive thoughts during sex?

How is my body showing stress or responding differently?

Have I noticed changes in my experience of self—such as numbing, depersonalization, hypersensitivity, or increased somatization?

Transforming the Pain: A Workbook on Vicarious Traumatization
Saakvitne, Pearlman, & Staff of TSI/CAAP (Norton, 1996)

Other Tools for Self-Assessment

In addition to the preceding worksheets, we have developed three measures that help identify signs of vicarious traumatization. These instruments examine specific beliefs and experiences. Each asks you to rate several statements or answer questions using a scaled answer (usually from 1 to 6). The result reflects your feelings and beliefs at that particular time. It can be helpful to fill out these questionnaires periodically to note changes over time and circumstances.*

The first measure is the TSI Belief Scale. This questionnaire asks about beliefs related to the five psychological needs. It is intended "to measure disruptions in beliefs about self and others which arise from psychological trauma or from vicarious exposure to trauma material through psychotherapy or other helping relationships" (Pearlman, in press). There are 80 questions and the rater is asked to indicate how much she or he agrees with each statement using a six-point scale.

The second measure, the Life Orientation Inventory (LOI), is a measure of spirituality developed by Debra Neumann and Laurie Pearlman (Neumann & Pearlman, in press). Again, this measure asks the rater to indicate the degree of agreement with 40 statements related to four dimensions of spirituality: nonmaterial aspects of life, meaning and hope, connection with something beyond oneself, and awareness of all aspects of life.

The third is a measure of self capacities being developed by Pamela Deiter and Laurie Pearlman. The Inner Experience Questionnaire (IEQ) measures affect tolerance, inner connection to others, and beliefs about the viability of the self (CSDT's "self capacities").

Measures such as these can provide more information about someone's beliefs and inner well-being. With this information you can

---

* See Pearlman & Saakvitne, 1995a, pp. 407–411, for the first two measures. To obtain the third measure, contact Dr. Laurie Pearlman, Director of Research, TSI/CAAP, 22 Morgan Farms Drive, South Windsor, CT 06074.

specify transformations within yourself and notice which changes are most distressing to you. Some will confirm what you already know (e.g., "I am more safety-conscious now than I used to be"), while some may come as a surprise to you (e.g., "I don't trust myself the way I used to"). There may be changes that you've noticed but did not connect to your work (e.g., "Lately, I feel more pessimistic about the world and people").

Ultimately, these assessment tools help you focus on areas for self-care and healing. First noticing your feelings, beliefs, and needs and then responding appropriately to them is the two-step approach to transforming vicarious traumatization. The next section is about assessing self-care patterns.

Assessing Self-Care

Given the physical, psychological, spiritual, and emotional stresses of our work, there isn't one of us who doesn't need to improve in some area of self-care. Caregivers are notoriously poor at self-care to begin with—and too often get worse rather than better as their work responsibilities increase.

Many caregivers only implement those types of self-care that directly help others (e.g., "I'll take time off when I am sick because that models self-care to my clients"). This philosophy reflects too narrow a definition of self: self as helper. Work is a part of life, but not its totality. We need a balance between work and leisure, action and reflection, giving and taking. We must embrace and integrate all of the many aspects of our selves. We are serious, playful, careful, spontaneous, sexual, intellectual, intense, self-indulgent, and much, much more. We are complex and we are human. Our self-care must reflect our diversity and complexity.

The following worksheet for assessing self-care is not exhaustive, merely suggestive. Feel free to add areas of self-care that are relevant for you and rate yourself on how often and how well you are taking care of yourself these days.

When you are finished, look for patterns in your responses. Are you more active in some areas of self-care but ignore others? Are there items on the list that make you think, "I would *never* do that"? Listen to your inner responses, your internal dialogue about self-care and making yourself a priority.

Self-Care

Rate the following areas in frequency
5 = Frequently
4 = Occasionally
3 = Rarely
2 = Never
1 = It never occurred to me

Physical Self-Care

_____ Eat regularly (e.g. breakfast, lunch, and dinner)

_____ Eat healthily

_____ Exercise

_____ Get regular medical care for prevention

_____ Get medical care when needed

_____ Take time off when sick

_____ Get massages

_____ Dance, swim, walk, run, play sports, sing, or do some other physical activity that is fun

_____ Take time to be sexual—with yourself, with a partner

_____ Get enough sleep

_____ Wear clothes you like

_____ Take vacations

_____ Take day trips or mini-vacations

_____ Make time away from telephones

_____ Other:

Psychological Self-Care

_____ Make time for self-reflection

_____ Have your own personal psychotherapy

_____ Write in a journal

Transforming the Pain: A Workbook on Vicarious Traumatization
Saakvitne, Pearlman, & Staff of TSI/CAAP (Norton, 1996)

_____ Read literature that is unrelated to work

_____ Do something at which you are not expert or in charge

_____ Decrease stress in your life

_____ Notice your inner experience—listen to your thoughts, judgments, beliefs, attitudes, and feelings

_____ Let others know different aspects of you

_____ Engage your intelligence in a new area, e.g., go to an art museum, history exhibit, sports event, auction, theater performance

_____ Practice receiving from others

_____ Be curious

_____ Say no to extra responsibilities sometimes

_____ Other:

Emotional Self-Care

_____ Spend time with others whose company you enjoy

_____ Stay in contact with important people in your life

_____ Give yourself affirmations, praise yourself

_____ Love yourself

_____ Reread favorite books, re-view favorite movies

_____ Identify comforting activities, objects, people, relationships, places and seek them out

_____ Allow yourself to cry

_____ Find things that make you laugh

_____ Express your outrage in social action, letters, donations, marches, protests

_____ Play with children

_____ Other:

Transforming the Pain: A Workbook on Vicarious Traumatization
Saakvitne, Pearlman, & Staff of TSI/CAAP (Norton, 1996)

Spiritual Self-Care

_____ Make time for reflection

_____ Spend time with nature

_____ Find a spiritual connection or community

_____ Be open to inspiration

_____ Cherish your optimism and hope

_____ Be aware of nonmaterial aspects of life

_____ Try at times not to be in charge or the expert

_____ Be open to not knowing

_____ Identify what is meaningful to you and notice its place in your life

_____ Meditate

_____ Pray

_____ Sing

_____ Spend time with children

_____ Have experiences of awe

_____ Contribute to causes in which you believe

_____ Read inspirational literature (talks, music, etc.)

_____ Other:

Workplace or Professional Self-Care

_____ Take a break during the workday (e.g., lunch)

_____ Take time to chat with co-workers

_____ Make quiet time to complete tasks

_____ Identify projects or tasks that are exciting and rewarding

_____ Set limits with clients and colleagues

_____ Balance your caseload so no one day or part of a day is "too much"

_____ Arrange your work space so it is comfortable and comforting

Transforming the Pain: A Workbook on Vicarious Traumatization
Saakvitne, Pearlman, & Staff of TSI/CAAP (Norton, 1996)

_____ Get regular supervision or consultation

_____ Negotiate for your needs (benefits, pay raise)

_____ Have a peer support group

_____ Develop a non-trauma area of professional interest

_____ Other:

Balance

_____ Strive for balance *within* your work-life and workday

_____ Strive for balance *among* work, family, relationships, play, and rest

Other Areas of Self-Care that are Relevant to You

Transforming the Pain: A Workbook on Vicarious Traumatization
Saakvitne, Pearlman, & Staff of TSI/CAAP (Norton, 1996)

Assessment Tools for Groups

When teaching groups of trauma workers about VT, we find it very useful to invite people to do a quick personal assessment using the exercise Making It Personal (see next page). It is a simple way to invite a group to examine their own experience of VT.

One person's list might say:

1. I don't watch the evening news anymore.

2. When my partner is late getting home, I fear the worst.

3. I cry easily at movies and even radio stories.

Another person's list might read:

1. I watch TV all the time, from the time I get home until I go to bed.

2. I go out less and when I do I no longer tell anyone what I do for a living.

3. Whenever I see a dad with a daughter, I worry he is a perpetrator.

Yet another might write:

1. I have really violent revenge fantasies about getting back at child abusers. They are disturbing because I don't see myself as a violent person.

2. I have bad dreams.

3. I have too little patience with my children—and I'm always scared for their safety so I'm overprotective.

This group introductory exercise can be a two-part exercise. The second part, Silent Witness, is a meaningful addition.

MAKING IT PERSONAL

Write down three signs of vicarious traumatization that you are aware of in your current life.

SILENT WITNESS

When asking people to list three signs of VT, let them know that you will ask them to show their list to others. Then after the lists are completed, say:

Now, I am going to ask you to stand and silently walk around the room. I invite you to share what you have written with one another, but do not comment or speak. We will do this for 5 (or 10) minutes.

Transforming the Pain: A Workbook on Vicarious Traumatization
Saakvitne, Pearlman, & Staff of TSI/CAAP (Norton, 1996)

The silent sharing in the second part is very powerful. It frees people to observe and acknowledge without needing to respond. It also demonstrates the power of bearing witness, which is an essential part of trauma work. The instruction to remain silent helps people stay focused on the powerful statements each has written, rather than nervously moving into social chatter.

We find that this exercise works well when the leader participates. This participation reinforces the message that we are all subject to VT and that it helps all of us to be open about it. It is also helpful for the leader; no matter how often we talk about VT, we can still be oblivious to our own.

Participants are often moved and saddened as well as relieved at the end of this exercise. When we invite feedback, we regularly hear:

- *"It was very validating."*
- *"I thought I was the only one who felt that way or had those thoughts."*
- *"I read things on other people's list that I could have written on mine."*

For this exercise and other participatory exercises, it is not unusual for people to feel shy initially. Many workplaces and professions reinforce punitive messages that it is shameful to acknowledge painful feelings or identify negative effects of our work. It is of course fine for anyone to remain seated and not participate. The leader may offer her list to some of them, and they may or may not share theirs. This exercise works even with very large groups. If the space does not easily allow movement or the time is very short, you can modify it by having people share their lists only with their immediate neighbors in the room.

At the end of the silent sharing, ask all who wish to do so to speak their observations or experience to the larger group (or in smaller groups if time and space permit). This discussion powerfully reinforces the experience of breaking the silence, an essential step in the ongoing process of transforming VT.

All of the assessment tools and exercises identified in this chapter provide essential information. By identifying specific areas of disruption and vulnerability, you can develop specific strategies for transformation and self-protection.

> Learning about VT I found (especially the Silent Witness exercise) to be very affirming and transforming. It helped me identify processes within myself that I was unaware were occurring. It made me realize how important it is for therapists to talk to each other about these issues, rather than to isolate with feelings of shame because we are human and imperfect. I left your workshop feeling renewed and full of hope. With this attitude I feel I can be a much more effective therapist and can enjoy my "other" life more.
>
> *—VT workshop participant, a psychologist in a rural practice*

Chapter 3
Addressing and Transforming Vicarious Traumatization

> Your reframing of our tears as natural and healthy expressions of the grief we must inevitably feel as a result of bearing witness to the pain of others has moved us to a deeper, personal understanding of this process. Thanks so much.
>
> *—VT workshop participants, administrators of a community mental health agency and organizers of the VT workshop*

Now you know what vicarious traumatization is and have some ways to identify and assess it. We turn at this point to how to address its impact. While we believe that the effects of vicarious traumatization are inevitable and permanent, we also believe they are modifiable. Thus, while this work *will* change you, there is a lot you can do about it. This chapter examines several general approaches to transforming vicarious traumatization; the next chapter contains specific exercises for individuals, pairs, and groups.

What Transforms Vicarious Traumatization?

There are two fundamental modes of approaching vicarious traumatization. The first focuses on the general need for better self-care and addresses the stress inherent in vicarious traumatization. The second focuses on the specific need for transformation of negative beliefs, despair, and loss of meaning and directly addresses the demoralization and loss of hope created by vicarious traumatization. *Antidotes for vicarious traumatization must address both stress and demoralization.*

In order to transform vicarious traumatization, you must love your work or some important aspect of your work. It must be more than a job. This work is too difficult and too personally demanding to do without a sense of mission or conviction. Without a passion for the work, an individual will most likely leave the field and move to a different type of work. In other words, your work must be meaningful to you. Then, paradoxically, your work itself is part of your antidote to vicarious traumatization. Certainly vicarious traumatization can obscure our love for the work, but once our energies are restored through supportive strategies, we should again feel our commitment to this work. If not, then it may be time to consider a change in focus, perhaps moving away from trauma work or reducing it in proportion to other work.

To Address the Stress of Vicarious Traumatization

General self-care strategies provide an essential component of addressing vicarious traumatization. In each realm of one's life there are strategies to improve the quality of that life and decrease the stress in it. We elaborate many of these later in this chapter. Self-care strategies fall into three categories: self-care, nurturing yourself, and escaping. Each of these strategies is useful and essential some of the time. Self-care includes balance, limits, healthy habits, and connection with others. Nurturing yourself includes gentleness, a focus on pleasure and comfort, relaxation, and play. Escape include activities that allow you to forget about work, to engage in fantasy, and to get away from painful feelings.

We can generate lists of ways to take better care of ourselves and create balance and connection at work and home. Yet these strategies alone will not help us to *transform* vicarious traumatization.

Addressing and Transforming VT

How to Address the Stress of VT

1. Self-care
2. Nurturing activities
3. Escape

How to Transform the Despair of VT

1. Create meaning
2. Infuse a current activity with meaning
3. Challenge your negative beliefs and assumptions (e.g., nihilism, cynicism, and despair)
4. Participate in community-building activities

To Transform Loss of Meaning by Vicarious Traumatization

The strategies that can allow us to transform vicarious traumatization are those that infuse meaning into our lives. These strategies inherently challenge the nihilism, despair, and cynicism that result from vicarious traumatization. They fall into four categories: creating meaning, infusing a current activity with meaning, challenging negative beliefs and assumptions, and community-building.

The first refers to the centrality of creating or discovering meaning. The making of meaning is the opposite of the erosion or negation of meaning that results from vicarious traumatization. Second, one can discover significance in already familiar activities by consciously infusing them with meaning, whether they be hobbies, playing with our children, reading philosophy, or civic commitments. For example, someone may be committed to daily exercise. But does that mean a reluctant trip to the gym, the greatest reward being its ending, or could it mean a cherished daily walk in the woods? The latter can be deeply meaningful when it includes reflection upon the beauty and miracles of nature, connection with a valued walking companion, intentional awareness of all of one's sensations during the course of the walk, and so forth. This kind of activity, mindful, intentional, and aware, actually helps us to transform vicarious traumatization by reconnecting us with ephemeral aspects of our experience, thereby restoring our spiritual awareness.

Third, any time you actively challenge or allow your experiences to challenge negative beliefs or cynicism, you are reclaiming meaning and transforming vicarious traumatization.

> *A trauma therapist told the following story:*
>
> "*I was driving in an unfamiliar rural area when I got a flat tire. I was in a hurry and wearing a light-colored dress, so I wasn't eager to change it myself. A pick-up truck pulled over a little way down the road and backed up. A man got out and walked toward me asking, 'Need any help?' I hesitated, flashing through story after story of assaults and struggling against stereotypical assumptions. Finally, smiling weakly, I accepted his offer. He quickly changed the tire and as he was putting the flat tire in the back of my car, he looked at me and said, 'There are good people in the world, you know.'*
>
> "*I realized that that was an 'anti-VT' experience—not primarily because some guy I'd mistrusted did a nice thing for me, but because he directly challenged my beliefs or assumptions. I felt real joy when he said that. I thought with relief, 'Yes, that's true. There are good people. The world is also a good place.'*"

Fourth, when you engage in community-building activities, in any community, small or large, you reclaim connection. Working together for a common goal or the common good offsets the psychic and spiritual isolation of vicarious traumatization.

The two modes, addressing and transforming, are not mutually exclusive. Protective behaviors can be meaningful activities. Meaningful activities can provide support and self-nurturance.

Awareness, Balance, and Connection

Three central aspects of all vicarious traumatization interventions are awareness, balance, and connection (what one colleague called the ABCs of VT). *Awareness* reflects our attunement to our own needs, limits, emotions, and resources. This awareness of one's own inner state and disequilibrium sets the stage for responsiveness and self-care. Full awareness requires attention to *all* aspects of one's experience, including dreams, imagination, associations, emotions, bodily sensations, and conscious and preconscious material. Awareness requires time and quiet for reflection; we will not be aware when we are always in action or sleep.

A trauma worker must have *balance,* both among life activities and within him- or herself. Balance provides stability to help you keep your footing and keep your priorities straight. Balancing work, play, and rest activities is an essential step. Inner balance requires mindfulness and awareness. This balance allows us to attend to all aspects of ourselves and thus be more integrated, complete people. It allows access to our inner resources and capacities for reflection and choice.

Maintaining *connection* to others, to ourselves, and to something larger than ourselves provides an antidote to the isolation that is a hallmark of vicarious traumatization. Inner connection allows us greater awareness of our needs, experience, and perception. Connection to others, personally and professionally, is critical for trauma workers; we cannot afford to do this work alone. To face the horrors of what we hear and witness we need our moorings. Our survivor clients often live in worlds peopled only by the brutal and the brutalized; if we, the helpers, don't stay connected to a larger, more complex world, we can

The ABCs of Addressing VT

Awareness

Being attuned to one's needs, limits, emotions, and resources. Heed all levels of awareness and sources of information, cognitive, intuitive, and somatic. Practice mindfulness and acceptance.

Balance

Maintaining balance among activities, especially work, play, and rest. Inner balance allows attention to all aspects of oneself.

Connection

Connections to oneself, to others, and to something larger. Communication is part of connection and breaks the silence of unacknowledged pain. These connections offset isolation and increase validation and hope.

In Three Realms Of Our Lives

- Professional
- Organizational
- Personal

get lost with them in a persecutory morass. It is the connection with something larger that provides an internal anchor for our experience. For some, this will be a god or other deity (e.g., God, Yahweh, Allah, Buddha, Goddess). For others, it may be nature, the universe, humanity, or life itself.

An important component of connection is communication. The expression or speaking of vicarious traumatization counteracts the insidious oppression of silence. It is in the speaking of our truth that we free ourselves, individually and collectively, to address our needs.

Mindfulness and Acceptance

Every intervention strategy for vicarious traumatization is predicated on mindfulness and acceptance. The first step in transforming vicarious traumatization is to *accept* it. Acceptance goes beyond recognition and awareness; it includes the deeper realization of the fundamental truth and inevitability of our inner changes and pain. The route to acceptance is through grief and struggle and the path afterwards is toward transformation. Acceptance incorporates grief. The process of grief involves denial and anger; our acceptance of vicarious traumatization will reflect a parallel struggle. Each of us wants to deny the transformation and to believe we have ultimate control over the process; these defenses preclude acceptance. Mindfulness—awareness and inner attunement—is an avenue for doing it differently.

Mindfulness is an old concept that is currently receiving new attention (Kabat-Zinn, 1994; Hanh, 1976; Linehan, 1993a, 1993b); it is an invaluable tool to counterbalance vicarious traumatization. Mindfulness is based on acceptance of what is in the moment without modification or judgment. Jon Kabat-Zinn writes,

> Fundamentally, mindfulness is a simple concept. Its power lies in its practice and its applications. Mindfulness means paying attention in a particular way: on purpose, in the present moment, and nonjudgmentally. This kind of attention nurtures greater awareness, clarity, and acceptance of present-moment reality. . . . Mindfulness provides a simple but powerful route for getting ourselves unstuck, back in touch

with our own wisdom and vitality. It is a way to take charge
of the direction and quality of our own lives, including our
own relationships within the family, our relationship to
work and to the larger world and planet, and, most fundamentally, our relationship with ourself as a person. . . . It is
the direct opposite of taking life for granted. (pp. 4-5)*

Mindfulness allows acceptance. It creates an inner equilibrium necessary for us to address our truth and remain grounded in the face of
the torrent of feelings and assaults to cherished beliefs that characterize
vicarious traumatization.

Realms of Intervention

There are three realms in which to address vicarious traumatization:
professional, organizational, and personal. Within each realm there are
a number of different strategies and interventions.

Professional Strategies

Awareness, balance, and connection serve a trauma worker well in the
professional realm. To begin with, it makes an enormous difference
simply to notice and acknowledge vicarious traumatization. When you
accept your responses as normal, you can more easily make space to
address them constructively. This awareness allows you to make active
choices to limit your exposure to traumatic material and to create balance in your work life.

Balance within the professional realm means both balance within
your caseload and among different professional tasks. Of course, in
each job the details of schedule and time allocation vary, but it is
important to consider your options. When you have the choice, it helps

---

* For more information on mindfulness practice and philosophy, see the works by
Jon Kabat-Zinn and Thich Nhat Hanh listed in the annotated bibliography.

not to see a caseload filled with survivors of the same type of trauma and to balance your caseload with clients with nontrauma-based issues to address. Limit how many clients with managed care review you accept. It can also make a big difference to limit the number of clients you see back-to-back. Given a choice, it is good to vary the rhythm of your day in order to have contact with colleagues and time for yourself. It is of great, often unrecognized, importance to take breaks during the day. In addition to physically mandated bathroom breaks, it helps to take a lunch break, time for a walk or other physical activity (including simply stretching or walking in a hallway), or even a nap.

Self-care at work is overlooked by many of us. Yet we have both physical and emotional needs at work too; we work better when those needs are met. Many of us sit very still all day, listening and working from our heads. We forget to move, to laugh, to listen to our bodies, and pay attention to our hearts.

Connection at work is about nurturing colleagueship. We cannot do this work alone; we need each other. In particular we need colleagues with whom we can be honest and vulnerable. Sharing our experience and hearing theirs offers validation and strengthens our resolve. We may speak to a friend in the field, a supervisor, or a group of colleagues. All trauma workers need places to talk about the feelings this work brings, including their countertransference and vicarious traumatization responses.

Everyone working with survivor clients needs supervision and consultation. Interpersonal relationships with survivors of interpersonal trauma are compelling and complicated. There are many potential pitfalls as we negotiate our clients' powerful needs and our own responses. This supervision should include an understanding of trauma and of the impact of vicarious traumatization on the helper. The table on the next page outlines the essential components of a trauma therapy supervision.*

---

* For discussion of models of trauma supervision, see Pearlman & Saakvitne (1995a, 1995b).

Key Components of Supervision for Trauma Therapies

- Theory, a clear theoretical orientation that incorporates conceptualizations of (1) the impact of trauma on psychological functioning as well as (2) psychotherapeutic technique and goals

- Education about symptom management and common posttraumatic stress and dissociative adaptations

- Focus on the therapeutic relationship

- Safety and respect to address countertransference

- Education about and attention to vicarious traumatization

There are many ways to maintain professional connection. Professional support or supervision groups can be organized with as few as two or three members. Professional trainings and conferences provide the opportunity to restore our sense of connection with others, to hear about others' work and successes, and to help us to normalize our responses to the work as we talk with colleagues who share these responses. Both the formal presentations and informal networking at such conferences provide opportunities for connection and sustenance.

Another forum for professional connection is in individual or group vicarious traumatization consultations. Such consultations allow trauma workers to talk about the feelings evoked by their work. For workers with their own history of trauma, a consultation can be a place to explore the ways in which personal history interacts with professional roles. It can be a place for helpers to identify the specific effects of their work on themselves, in the context of each one's particular frame of reference, emotional style, and salient need areas. These groups provide an invaluable forum for validation, reality testing, problem-solving, and clinical supervision.

Again, professional strategies are most likely to be effective if you fundamentally value and love your work. That cannot be prescribed, although it can be enhanced by the strategies we have just outlined. If this is a question for you, take time to examine your priorities and values as they are met or not met in your work. The work needs to be inherently rewarding at some level to balance the enormous costs that come with it. If after examination this remains a question for you, it is probably wise to seek a consultation to explore this further.

Organizational Strategies

The ideas around dealing with VT professionally and organizationally will be quite valuable for a team of people who work together, have some processes in place to support one another, but can now take this much further.

—*VT workshop participant, a member of the inpatient staff at a private psychiatric hospital*

There are many things an organization can do to protect its workers—and therefore its clients and itself—from the negative effects of trauma work. For example, physical space is important; when the physical space conveys safety, respect (e.g., soundproofing for consultation rooms or therapy offices), comfort, and beauty, the message is one of hope and esteem.

Organizations can ensure that all clinical staff members have adequate supervision and consultation. The organization benefits from the improved services and protection against poor or dangerous practices that can occur when work with trauma survivors occurs in isolation.

The best financial security a service organization can have is excellence in service.

When organizations provide resources and support for continuing education, the caliber of the work at the organization improves. Medical policies that offer reasonable coverage for mental health benefits are a necessity for workers in the field of trauma. Adequate pay and time off are also a necessity; nobody can do this work well and safely without resources and time for replenishment and self-care.

Some organizational supports require the allocation of funds. Many, however, simply require an attitude of respect for the difficulty of the work and a commitment to address the potential for harm to workers and clients. Organizations that serve traumatized clients must acknowledge the impact of vicarious traumatization on their employees and identify strategies for protecting and healing workers. Often, a first step is recognition of the central role of trauma in the lives of many mental health service consumers. The corollary is to understand that psychopathology often has its roots in adaptations to psychological trauma.

Making time to address vicarious traumatization is important both symbolically and pragmatically. Symbolically, time allocation underscores the importance of the issue of vicarious traumatization. Pragmatically, talking about and addressing vicarious traumatization decreases its effects. Using all or part of staff meetings to address vicarious traumatization will make a significant difference. At TSI/CAAP we do this weekly; some organizations offer such meetings biweekly or even monthly. Staff retreats are also useful forums in which to explore and address vicarious traumatization.

A Note to Administrators

Administrators of agencies that serve trauma survivors often have extraordinarily difficult jobs balancing the needs of clients, their staff, and their fiscal limitations and responsibilities. Administrators often have to answer to other authorities who do not understand trauma work or its effects on the helper. In nonprofit or public service organizations, administrators may have to answer to boards of directors, government officials, and sometimes the general public. In for-profit or corporate organizations, they may have to answer to CEOs, managers, or executives with very different goals. They are also then subject to an additional level of stress and potential vicarious traumatization: They must witness their staff's struggles and then feel either effective or ineffective in offering support and protection. When administrators participate in VT exercises, they often process them on two levels, both as individuals and on behalf of the organization and staff as a whole.

Personal Strategies

The most important strategy in your personal life is to have one. Your personal life must be a priority, which is another way of saying that *you* must be a priority. Trauma work is often compelling and too many of us manage the demands by giving and giving and making work the center of our lives. It's fine if your work is compelling to you, but it's not fine if it is *all* of your life; both the quality of your life and your work will suffer. Not taking time for a personal life provides a poor model to your clients and deprives you of your complexity and humanity.

In your personal life it is important to be in roles that differ from your professional personae. If you are a caretaker at work and a parent at home, it is important to set aside time to be a painter, a poet, a lover, a hedonist, a gardener, a person of leisure. When your work requires you to be thoughtful and careful, it's important to have places in which you can be spontaneous, unreasonable, frivolous, silly, irreverent. You need time to play, to be carefree, to have no responsibility, to be in complete control, and to have no control.

Your personal life also needs balance. You need to balance the different parts of you and your life, including the spiritual, physical, emotional, relational, psychological, creative, and sensual parts. There is not time in every day for everything, but there is time in every life for all of you to be nurtured and explored.

Resources in your personal life may include personal psychotherapy, a spiritual community, other kinds of healing activities such as massage therapy, yoga, acupuncture, exercise classes, and others. Friends, family, and neighbors are other resources. Cultural, recreational, and nature centers and events are more resources. Your children and those of friends and family may be resources for play and perspective.

Rest and play are two often overlooked essentials of life for a trauma worker. Discover what is restful for you. It may be an afternoon in the hammock, a jigsaw puzzle, a dozen mysteries, a day at the beach. Have you laughed heartily in the last week? What makes you laugh? What makes you chuckle or grin? What daydreams do you enjoy? How well do you know your playful self?

Attention to meaning making in your personal life occurs in spiritual realms, as you become more aware and centered in everyday activities, as you make conscious choices and attend to the meaning of those choices, or as you participate in and build community.

Research Findings on Helpful Activities

Two recent studies asked mental health professionals about activities they engaged in to balance their trauma work. In the first study (Pearlman & Mac Ian, 1995), almost 200 trauma therapists (mostly women) found the following activities helpful: discussing cases with colleagues, attending workshops, spending time with family or friends, traveling, vacation, hobbies, movies, socializing, exercising, and limiting their caseloads. In the second study (Gamble, Pearlman, Lucca, & Allen, 1994), over 100 psychologists (mostly men) found the following activities helpful: taking vacations, engaging in social activities, obtaining

VT Intervention Strategies for Each Realm of the Helper's Life

Professional
- Supervision/consultation
- Scheduling: client load and distribution
- Balance and variety of tasks
- Education: giving and receiving
- Work space

Organizational
- Collegial support
- Forums to address VT
- Supervision availability
- Respect for clinicians and clients
- Resources: mental health benefits, space, time

Personal
- Making personal life a priority
- Personal psychotherapy
- Leisure activities: physical, creative, spontaneous, relaxation
- Spiritual well-being
- Nurture all aspects of yourself: emotional, physical, spiritual, interpersonal, creative, artistic
- Attention to health

In All Realms
- Mindfulness and self-awareness
- Self-nurturance
- Balance: work, play, rest
- Meaning and connection

emotional support from colleagues, friends, and family, pleasure and professional reading, seeking consultation on difficult cases, taking breaks during the workday, spending time with children, listening to music, spending time in nature, and attending workshops or conferences.

What About Intrusive Imagery?

It is not uncommon for trauma workers to be troubled by disturbing intrusive imagery from clients' material. These images can come during the day, during sex, or in nightmares; they may be mainly visual or they may include auditory experiences, bodily sensations, smells, or emotional responses to certain cues (e.g., basements, stairwells, bathrooms). They are often hard to talk about and frequently disturbing. Often they are related to a specific scene we have heard described or implied, something we have seen in photographs, or a painful reenactment in our work.

Acknowledging the intrusive image is the first step. There are several things that can be helpful. One is to discuss it with a trusted colleague or therapist. The process of sharing it may diminish its potency for two reasons. One, as you speak, it ceases to be a secret and you share the pain with another. Two, as you come to understand why this particular image or sensation is staying with you, you will connect it to other familiar aspects of yourself. What does it trigger in you? What salient needs of yours are represented by this particular image—loss of safety, lack of control, betrayal of trust, shame or humiliation (loss of esteem), abandonment (loss of intimacy)? Does the need area represented make sense to you; that is, given what you know of yourself, can you understand why this image in particular might stay with you?

If speaking and insight do not relieve the intrusion, you may find it helpful to use guided imagery. You may need to transform the image or sensation by consciously evoking it and then gradually transforming it by adding or subtracting elements until it becomes a scene under your control and through which you can reestablish the need represented. Sometimes this can be accomplished by empowering yourself or someone else in the image (gaining superhuman strength, you are able to hurl the potential attacker some five miles hence into a crocodile-infested swamp), using the ridiculous (transform the threatening villain into a toad on stilts), or incorporating the spiritual (you or the child become enveloped in a protective white cloud that no one can penetrate). You will need to experiment to find what imagery transformation fits the underlying needs and anxieties represented by the particular image.

In this chapter, we have been discussing *general* ways to prevent or lessen the impact of vicarious traumatization. Another set of vicarious traumatization interventions are *specifically* designed to address certain aspects of vicarious traumatization. These interventions or exercises take a variety of forms, but all aim to increase the trauma worker's awareness, balance, and connection with him or herself and others. Chapter 4 describes several such interventions.

Chapter 4

Exercises for Individuals, Dyads, and Groups

It was wonderful to know that others are experiencing the same.

—*VT workshop participant, a counselor in a partial hospital chemical dependency program*

This chapter offers a selection of exercises that we have found helpful in addressing various aspects of vicarious traumatization.* With each exercise we provide a brief introduction explaining its application and identifying the aspects of vicarious traumatization it addresses. We present most of these exercises as they would be used in a group. However, many can be adapted for dyads or for individual use.

Try to approach each exercise with an open mind. You cannot know going into an exercise what will come of it. Often participants find that the meaning of an exercise is not apparent until some time later. Others are surprised at insight they gain even while feeling skeptical. Our cynicism can mislead us. Out of our need not to feel vulnerable or not to cry, we close our hearts and minds. This defensiveness may parallel that of our clients and give us new appreciation for their fears, but it does not serve us well in the long run. Like our clients we must risk hope in order to heal.

---

* Our selection is by no means an exhaustive list. We offer an annotated bibliography at the end of the workbook for other sources that provide useful exercises and strategies.

Mind, Body, Experience: Think, Act, Feel

Vicarious traumatization interventions engage mind, body, and/or experience; that is, they invite the participant to think, act, or feel something in order to deepen his or her awareness, enhance the connection with self and others, and increase the balance in work and personal life.

Thinking exercises often ask the participant to catalog signs of vicarious traumatization or develop strategies for addressing vicarious traumatization and improving self-care. *Body exercises* often involve exercise, relaxation, or activity. They serve to increase the participant's awareness of his or her body and the impact of vicarious traumatization on the body (stress, tension), and to identify resources for self-care and connection to self and nature. *Experiential exercises* invite the participant to be in touch with his or her feelings, often through guided imagery, art, writing, or music.

Each of these approaches serves to increase the participant's self-knowledge and affect tolerance. These exercises are usually followed by a discussion in which participants can share some aspect of their experience, thus often decreasing their isolation. The exercises in this chapter are organized according to this loose template of mind, body, experience; clearly these three categories are interconnected.

Guidelines For Vicarious Traumatization Group Exercises

As in any group or consultation, safety is the first order of business. Participants should be told ahead of time what the exercise entails. They need to be reminded that participation is voluntary; any participant can decline to participate, stop at any time, decide to observe only, or do an exercise privately—that is, without participating in any discussion. It is helpful to clarify any rules about confidentiality; we request that participants agree to a rule of confidentiality about the exercise and ensuing discussion. Each participant is asked to be respectful of the process and not interrupt or disrupt it. Ideally, the boundaries should be set such that there will be no interruptions (no phone calls, no beepers, and no entrances or interruptions once an exercise begins). If an interruption is anticipated it should be acknowledged ahead of time.

Sometimes vicarious traumatization exercises bring up strong feelings. We recommend you have boxes of tissues readily available; it is normal and often healing for participants to cry during VT exercises. When an exercise is incorporated into a meeting during a workday, or a workshop is a half-day and people plan to work afterward, participants need time to process and unwind before returning to "work mode."

When someone is in the midst of a current personal trauma or loss or engaged in intensive therapeutic work on issues of childhood trauma, or when a particular exercise may elicit too great a feeling of vulnerability for a given individual, vicarious traumatization issues may be better addressed in individual therapy. Each participant will need to determine his or her own level of comfort and safety.

Mind: Thinking Exercises

Thinking exercises invite the participant to think about vicarious traumatization and its components. When you ask participants to identify signs of vicarious traumatization, or identify ameliorative strategies they could use in their professional, personal, and organizational contexts, you are asking them to think. Assessment tools such as those discussed in chapter 2 generally fit into this category. Whenever you ask participants to think or write an answer to a question or a list, let them know ahead of time whether they will be asked to share their thoughts. Some exercises work best if shared (Silent Witness); others are primarily private (Personal Vulnerabilities); and others allow a choice for those who wish to share something of their experience or thoughts.

Introductions

To start a vicarious traumatization workshop or group exercise, it is useful to invite participants to introduce themselves, for example:

> **To introduce yourself, please tell us your name and the kind of work you do. Then identify (a) what is most rewarding about your current work and (b) what is most stressful or distressing about your work at present.**

or

> **Remember why you entered this field. What did you hope to accomplish? What negative outcomes did you anticipate?**

The first introduction invites participants to connect with and assess their professional selves. The second invites them to think developmentally about themselves as professionals by remembering their goals and fears when they entered the field—which provides a context for reflections on their current experience. By speaking aloud, the introductions begin to break down the barriers of silence and isolation within which so many of us work. The introductions can serve to set a tone for self-reflection and sharing, which model the tasks of a vicarious traumatization intervention or workshop.

Transforming vicarious traumatization requires both self-awareness and connection with others. By sharing your experiences and realizations, you deepen your own awareness and enhance that of others. Thus group settings for vicarious traumatization interventions can be extraordinarily powerful and validating.

Vicarious Traumatization Assessment

Making It Personal, a common group assessment tool used at workshops where participants are being introduced to the concept of vicarious traumatization, is described on page 68. Participants are asked to identify three signs of vicarious traumatization in their lives. Specifically, they are invited to notice changes in their daily lives—social, leisure, contemplative, spiritual, or professional—and to write down three of these. As noted earlier, this exercise is generally followed by an experiential component, Silent Witness, in which participants walk around the room silently sharing their lists.

Strategies to Address Vicarious Traumatization

The following ten pages present specific thinking exercises designed to help participants address and contextualize their own vicarious traumatization. Several exercises focus on developing personal strategies to address VT. They invite individuals or groups to brainstorm, along various dimensions, potential useful strategies for addressing and transforming vicarious traumatization. These exercises include Addressing and Transforming VT, Making a Commitment to Yourself, Write Yourself a Letter, and Evaluate Your Personal VT Plan, and are presented on the next four pages.

A thinking exercise can be any task, individual or group, that invites helpers to consider their needs, evaluate their resources, and identify the impact of their work on themselves. "Seven More Thinking Exercises" is a list of several examples of questions and tasks that invite such reflection and lead to greater insight and self-awareness.

Many thinking exercises lend themselves well to group discussion. Success Stories and Creativity in Your Life are two exercises that provide good starting points for discussion. Your Professional Lifeline, the last exercise in this secion, asks participants to look at VT as a developmental process. These last three exercises begin on page 100.

ADDRESSING AND TRANSFORMING VT

This exercise helps people distinguish between addressing and transforming vicarious traumatization. Each participant will leave the exercise with several specific suggestions for him- or herself.

Using a flip chart to write down the ideas, the leader first asks the group to brainstorm together:

What can you do to address and lessen your stress level? What strategies for self-care, nurture, or escape do you use?

After collecting suggestions from the participants, the leader asks:

In what way do any of these strategies also transform VT? What else can you do to transform the pain of VT? How can you find meaning, imbue familiar activities with meaning, challenge negative beliefs, or participate with others in community-building?

Items from the first list may include:

> playing ball with my kids
> reading in the hammock
> gardening
> swimming
> singing in church choir
> watching TV
> not watching TV

The second list may include items like:

> playing with my kids, enjoying their curiosity and security
> walking in the woods and noticing the beauty
> going to temple
> participating in protest marches
> having neighborhood potluck dinners
> gardening
> meditation

Transforming the Pain: A Workbook on Vicarious Traumatization
Saakvitne, Pearlman, & Staff of TSI/CAAP (Norton, 1996)

MAKING A COMMITMENT TO YOURSELF

1. Write down three things you could do to address vicarious traumatization for each arena: professional, organizational, and personal.

Professional

1. _____
2. _____
3. _____

Organizational

1. _____
2. _____
3. _____

Personal

1. _____
2. _____
3. _____

2. Next, place an asterisk beside every strategy you could implement during the next month.

3. Then, circle one in each category that you will try to do during the next week.

The lists might look like the following:

Personal

1. take a vacation
2. exercise *
3. have lunch with a close friend *

Professional

1. go for a walk *
2. schedule supervision *
3. take a break after 3 sessions

Organizational

1. have VT discussions *
2. reading/discussion group
3. staff party *

Transforming the Pain: A Workbook on Vicarious Traumatization
Saakvitne, Pearlman, & Staff of TSI/CAAP (Norton, 1996)

Exercise

WRITE YOURSELF A LETTER

An effective follow-up to any VT workshop in general, and the Making a Commitment to Yourself exercise in particular, is to have participants write themselves a letter in which they remind themselves of what they have learned in the workshop and make a commitment to address and transform VT in specific ways. Ask them to address an envelope to themselves and place the letter in it. Then, collect the letters and mail them to participants at a set date 4 to 6 months later. (Remember to include envelopes with your workshop materials.)

Transforming the Pain: A Workbook on Vicarious Traumatization
Saakvitne, Pearlman, & Staff of TSI/CAAP (Norton, 1996)

EVALUATE YOUR PERSONAL VT PLAN

This exercise helps you evaluate your VT game plan. The instructions are:

After generating a list of strategies that you might use to address your own VT, review the list with the following questions in mind:

1. Does this activity primarily allow me to escape my feelings about the work?

2. Can I create new meaning from or about this activity?

3. Could this activity be an opportunity for connection with something larger than myself? for an awareness of other aspects of life?

4. How would it be to do this activity with full awareness of what I'm doing while I'm doing it? of my body and all of my sensations?

Transforming the Pain: A Workbook on Vicarious Traumatization
Saakvitne, Pearlman, & Staff of TSI/CAAP (Norton, 1996)

SEVEN MORE THINKING EXERCISES

Here are instructions for additional thinking exercises. Be sure each participant has writing materials.

Personal Vulnerabilities

Each of us works within our own historical and current circumstances, professional and personal situations, and our own temperament and emotional style. For example, some of us have children, some have personal trauma histories, some are new to the work or new to trauma work specifically, some work in unsupportive work environments, some have too little control over some aspects of our work or no safe place to talk about the work and its effects on us, some of us have current personal crises that demand our attention and deplete our energy. Take some time to jot down what in your present or past, personal or professional life might contribute to your vulnerability. This is for your use only.

Wish List for Your Organization

If your organization recognized VT and had a commitment to address it, what would be different? What policies, structures, and resources would you need? What values would need to change?

The Best of All Possible Worlds

If you had all the resources you needed to help you do your work, what would you need and want? Imagine the ideal work situation for you and your work.

Personal Resource List

Make a list of your current resources. Include internal and external resources, people, places, or things that are hope-giving, spirit-renewing, creative, playful, loving, woman-affirming, man-affirming, child-affirming, society-affirming. Choose some things that include your body, health, voice, tears, laughter, connection, silence, and spontaneity. This is an opportunity to identify what you have and may be underutilizing.

Transforming the Pain: A Workbook on Vicarious Traumatization
Saakvitne, Pearlman, & Staff of TSI/CAAP (Norton, 1996)

Rewards of Your Work

Make a list of the rewards of your work. How have you grown and changed in positive ways? What have you learned? What has moved you? How have you made a difference to others? What successes have you and your clients shared? What has made you laugh? Reread this list and add to it regularly.

Identify Your Needs

Make two columns. On the left list ways you experience vicarious traumatization at work or at home (include intrusive imagery). After you've completed that list, use the right-hand column to identify the need area represented by the disruption. That is, does this sign represent a disruption in your need for (a) safety, (b) trust, (c) esteem, (d) control, (e) intimacy, (f) or in your frame of reference (identity, world view, and spirituality), or some combination of these?

How Are You Meeting Your Needs?

Using the previous exercise as a starting point, list the needs that seem most impacted by your work. Under each need, list three ways you currently get that need met. Finally, for each need area, identify one strategy for meeting the need differently or for restoring or healing the disrupted belief.

Transforming the Pain: A Workbook on Vicarious Traumatization
Saakvitne, Pearlman, & Staff of TSI/CAAP (Norton, 1996)

SUCCESS STORIES

Some of the rewards of our work come from the fact that people who have been traumatized get better when given an opportunity to talk about and understand their experience. In both small and monumental ways, the work we do changes the lives of the people with whom we work. Too often we are distracted from these accomplishments by a seemingly endless stream of crises and needs.

Ask the group to talk about recent successes, to think of the client who made it through the weekend without drugs or alcohol, the client who called a friend for support, the family who got to the safety of a shelter, the crisis call that came in time, the interaction in which both people listened. The ensuing discussion will emphasize the hope and mastery in the work we do. This opportunity to experience hope and wonder together with colleagues renews us spiritually and professionally.

Remember that these successes are also our work and they sustain us. On a regular basis (perhaps weekly) make time with colleagues, or alone, to identify and enjoy your successes.

Transforming the Pain: A Workbook on Vicarious Traumatization
Saakvitne, Pearlman, & Staff of TSI/CAAP (Norton, 1996)

CREATIVITY IN YOUR LIFE

Ask people to come to the group with a "show and tell" item that indicates something creative in their lives that renews them. Specifically, the item should identify one way the participant (does or could) uses creative means to heal or express him- or herself, or to play.

When we did this exercise at a staff retreat, some of the items that were presented included:

photographs of a garden
an African drum
sheet music from a choral group
beautifully painted woodwork projects
music (Motown—to which we all were invited to dance!)
recordings and lyrics of "healing" songs

Transforming the Pain: A Workbook on Vicarious Traumatization
Saakvitne, Pearlman, & Staff of TSI/CAAP (Norton, 1996)

YOUR PROFESSIONAL LIFELINE

The purpose of this exercise is to help participants gain a historical perspective on the inner changes (both positive and negative) that have occurred since beginning their careers.

The materials you will need are: magic markers (at least 3 colors per person), a few feet of paper (computer paper or rolls of paper work well), and some space to spread out the paper.

The instructions are as follows:

Most of us wanted to be in our profession, to be helpers, because we were idealistic, oriented toward social activism, or deeply concerned with and connected to people. Generally we didn't enter this line of work primarily to make money, although we hope to be able to make a living from it, but because the work was compelling or interesting to us. Just as your clients have grown and changed as you worked with them, so too you have undergone developmental changes.

On the sheet in front of you, draw a horizontal line across the middle of the sheet. This line indicates the time span from when you first decided to go into this work. (For some of us, that decision came fairly early in life; for others, it occurred in adulthood after experimenting with other vocations.) At the leftmost end of the line, write the year you decided you wanted to be a helping professional. At the rightmost end, write this year.

Now mark the intervening years. You may want to make the intervals evenly spaced, or, if some years seem longer than others, the intervals can reflect that.

On the left end of the line, in whatever colors fit, write the adjectives to describe who you were the year you decided to enter this field. You might describe yourself, your personality, the innate helping skills you brought to your vision of yourself in your future career. Think of a phrase to describe your frame of reference (world view) at that time and write it in.

Transforming the Pain: A Workbook on Vicarious Traumatization
Saakvitne, Pearlman, & Staff of TSI/CAAP (Norton, 1996)

Now, for the intervening years, I want you to do two things:

1. Above the line, write in events and milestones in your professional life; write these events (e.g., started school, first job) above the approximate year they occurred.

2. Below the line, in a different color, write in important personal events and milestones (relationships beginning or ending, births, deaths, moves, transitions) and times of crisis or particular growth.

Now, reflect on particular clients with whom you've worked over the years. Who are the individuals who have had a real impact on you as a therapist and as a person? These may be some of your most difficult clients or some of your most enjoyable clients, those who taught you the most, who did the best, or those who hurt or discouraged you the most, clients who took a toll on you, clients who inspired you. These people have changed you and stayed with you internally, as your reservoir of professional experience. On your timeline write the initials of these clients at the year or years when you worked with them.

Now, at the right end, by today's date, write in a description of yourself today. Include also a phrase or sentence describing your current world view.

Finally, by yourself or with a partner, examine the timeline.

- What similarities or differences do you notice about the professional and personal events?

- What interplay do you see among your personal transitions and developmental milestones and the clients who have most affected you?

- What hypotheses come to mind?

- Compare your two world views. In what way have they changed? Is that a result of your work? Do they reflect vicarious traumatization?

Transforming the Pain: A Workbook on Vicarious Traumatization
Saakvitne, Pearlman, & Staff of TSI/CAAP (Norton, 1996)

Body: Action Exercises

Body exercises encourage participants to become more aware of their physical experience and needs. These exercises can be done individually, with a partner, or in a group. Goals include greater attunement to one's body, improved physical self-care, play, self-soothing, and connection with nature. Relaxation strategies and "safe place" imagery, breathing exercises and meditations, and physically active exercises such as walking, hiking, swimming, stretching, yoga, dancing, drumming, and so forth are included in this category.

Movement Exercises

An *extended yoga session* can be a vicarious traumatization exercise when it is done in the context of recognizing that we work with clients whose bodies have been battered, who treat their bodies with brutality or neglect, who have experienced traumatic assaults to their previously healthy bodies. As we sit with survivors and listen to their stories, our bodies can become tense and come to hold their pain and immobility. As we work to reconnect with our bodies and feel their strength and health, we balance the negative messages we hear about bodies from our clients. We then reenter our work with renewed commitment to people's right to healthy relationships with their bodies.

A *drumming session* can allow us to connect kinesthetically and viscerally with deep and basic feelings. Group drumming allows connection with others as we match and weave rhythms together. Drumming can be an expression of outrage and determination, as is the drumming session that concludes each meeting of the Eastern Regional Conference on Trauma, Abuse, and Dissociation, which is entitled "Drumming Out Abuse."

Dancing, whether slow and interpretive or boisterous and playful, integrates movement and music and, if done with others, connection and communication. It reminds us of the many ways we experience and respond to the world; it integrates different senses and sensations, allowing us again to be physical and fully responsive.

Nature and Senses

Nature is a major source of healing from vicarious traumatization. Being out-of-doors can provide serenity that restores us and a perspective that calms us. The timeless beauty helps us reconnect with the natural world and its inherent healing power. Nature is experienced through all sensory modalities and reminds us to listen to all our senses.

Touch, Look, Listen is an exercise that encourages participants to be fully aware in a natural setting (see next page). When we did this exercise at TSI/CAAP, weeks later several people noted that they had held onto the reminder that nature was a powerful "anti-VT" resource just outside their doors. Some had made a point to go to parks and on hikes over the subsequent weeks.

Some exercises involve symbolic action that can be both playful and powerful. Toxic Waste Dump and Reclaiming Life and Laughter are two examples (see page 107). The power of symbolic action is evident in such national projects as the AIDS Memorial Quilt (The Names Project) and The Clothesline Project. Both of these memorials to those who have died and/or been abused express grief and mourning while celebrating creativity and connection. These symbols remind us not to forget and not to be silent.

TOUCH, LOOK, LISTEN

Invite a group of trauma workers to convene at a nearby park or natural setting. Ask them to form three groups, and then give each group a "wilderness kit." One kit should include a tape recorder and the following instructions:

Enjoy your walk with an ear to the ground and to the sky. Notice the various sounds around you. Return to the group with a collection of different interesting things to listen to, using the tape recorder to capture sounds you are unable to share more directly.

The second kit should contain a Polaroid camera with these instructions:

Enjoy your walk, paying special attention to the sights around you . . . colors, angles, textures, shapes, shadows, etc. Return to the group with a collection of different visual impressions and objects that you found most interesting.

The third kit has simply the following instructions:

Enjoy your walk, focusing on your tactile experience, how things feel to the touch . . . sharp, soft, hard, rough, smooth, etc. Return to the group with a collection of different interesting things to touch/feel.

Ask the groups to meet at a central meeting place in 20 minutes to share their particular sensory experience of the walk.

Transforming the Pain: A Workbook on Vicarious Traumatization
Saakvitne, Pearlman, & Staff of TSI/CAAP (Norton, 1996)

TOXIC WASTE DUMP

This exercise was described by Guzzino and Taxis (1995), two therapists who run an experiential vicarious traumatization group for professionals. During their groups they use a large covered plastic bin plastered with warning signs about its lethal content, called the "toxic waste dump."

The symbolic dumping site is placed in the center of the group. Group participants are then invited to release their toxic stories into the bin, sometimes silently, sometimes with a eulogy. Participants create symbolic representations by, for example, drawing a painful feeling or symptom of VT, or by writing down an unbearable story, an ugly truth, or a defeating belief. They then rid themselves of these traumatically toxic stories or images by releasing or disposing of them, by symbolically throwing them away.

RECLAIMING LIFE AND LAUGHTER

The above exercise can be followed by a ceremony of reclaiming. As part of creating meaning, and thus transforming vicarious traumatization, there are several ways to reaffirm life and hope after letting go of pain and despair. Group members can offer an action or ritual of healing to follow the ritual of release.

For example, participants can light a candle to reclaim the light of truth, or sing or cheer to reclaim their voices. They can identify a source of pleasure to reclaim their bodies and to reclaim joy. The group can share healthy food to reclaim that which is healthy and sustains life, or give something symbolic of healing and health to one another to reclaim healing connections.

Transforming the Pain: A Workbook on Vicarious Traumatization
Saakvitne, Pearlman, & Staff of TSI/CAAP (Norton, 1996)

Experience: Feeling Exercises

> Experiential exercises are extremely valuable for me because they call me to define what this is for me and empower me to discover what I need to do.
>
> *—VT workshop participant, an expressive arts therapist working in a residential school for troubled adolescents*

Experiential exercises invite participants to notice and address feelings related to vicarious traumatization. They are designed to evoke and then integrate feelings with healing imagery. Several of these exercises draw from specific creative arts therapy techniques.

Guzzino and Taxis (1995) discuss the value of both psychodrama and art therapy techniques, with the caveat that they are powerful tools for which one needs specialized training. The techniques we suggest here do not constitute psychodrama or art therapy, but are exercises designed to be employed in a respectful, bounded way for the purpose of self-exploration and the amelioration of vicarious traumatization.

Sculpture Techniques

Sculpture techniques draw upon psychodrama, dance, and family therapy approaches. One example is Creating a Self-Sculpture (see page 110).

Guzzino and Taxis (1995) describe the following similar sculpting exercise used in a vicarious trauma group:

> In one session, participants were asked to work in pairs with one person acting as a piece of unformed clay. Here the protagonist molds the clay into a sculpture of a current vicariously traumatic experience. One participant silently sculpted her partner into a kneeling posture with hands covering eyes. Through this, the sculptor was able to connect with her feelings of despair, vulnerability, and hope-

lessness. Gradually, fears of being unable to see an imaginary attacker arose. We then instructed the sculptor to mold the antithesis of the first sculpture. The sculptor molded a standing figure, hands on hips, able to see and move in all directions. Feelings of power and strength increased for the sculptor. By changing the position of kneeling and vulnerability to standing and empowerment, the sculptor built a bridge between her vicarious trauma and healing. The protagonist was able to witness this transformation repeatedly until it became consciously internalized as an evolutionary process. (p. 28)

Experiential exercises require a respectful format that allows for initial connection, necessary instructions, the exercise, the processing of the work, and wrap-up and unwinding to allow for transition out of the exercise or group to other matters. Guzzino and Taxis structure their monthly groups so that each three-hour group includes a warm-up phase, experiential work, integration, and closure.

They suggest other sculpting techniques as group-building activities, for example, "introducing oneself through images representing one's professional vs. personal life, or by taking the role of a favorite office furnishing that describes the professional who owns it" (p. 28).

CREATING A SELF-SCULPTURE

In this exercise, group members work in pairs. Each participant is asked to "sculpt" her partner into a representative image of herself as a psychotherapist. The partner relaxes her body and allows the "sculptor" to move her into position. This exercise is done with as little talk as necessary. By literally putting her partner in her own experience, the sculptor shares her experience in a kinesthetic way. She can see her internal experience as she views her sculpted partner. After both partners have the opportunity to sculpt each other, the group re-forms and each member presents her sculpture. This viewing is followed by a discussion of the exercise and the feelings it evoked.

Transforming the Pain: A Workbook on Vicarious Traumatization
Saakvitne, Pearlman, & Staff of TSI/CAAP (Norton, 1996)

Art Techniques

Art therapy presents another modality for experiential exercises. Artwork can be used in vicarious traumatization exercises in a variety of ways. Guzzino and Taxis (1995) make the point, "Often, group members find that before the healing process can begin, the vicarious trauma must first be concretized visually. . . . Through the creation of artwork, participants can transform their vicarious trauma by changing the images and constructing additional resources" (pp. 28-29). Color and Transformation, Draw-a-Tree Series,* and its variation, Trees Across the Work Day, are three vicarious traumatization exercises that use art techniques; these are presented on the next four pages.

---

* We thank Sandra Streifender, M.A., for the tree exercises described in this chapter.

COLOR AND TRANSFORMATION

This exercise requires two facilitators. While one facilitator is giving directions, the other is spreading out various art materials, paper and pens, crayons, markers, and pastels of different colors.

Transition into exercise

I'd like to ask you to close your eyes—taking this time to turn inward—leaving behind the details of the day, the planning, agendas, time tables, schedules, and appointments—shifting to a place of feelings and impressions. Breathe deeply and work toward an inner focus. Now, while maintaining your inward focus, I'd like you slowly to open your eyes, keeping your gaze soft, and looking around at the colors and materials around you. Focus on the colors and your inner response to them—select some colors to which you feel drawn at the moment. Throughout this experience, you will be able to shift your choice of colors, depending on how your feelings shift from one moment to the next. Pick up a piece of paper and settle back into your seat, remaining in a place of inner focus. Close your eyes and allow yourself to become aware of what you are feeling.

Exercise

I'm going to guide you through a series of three drawing experiences which will help connect you with your experience of your work through your creative process.

1. Now take a moment to remember how you feel at times when you are feeling most yourself, the way you most like to feel as a therapist, or as the essential you, times when you feel relaxed, creative, active, open, reflective. You may focus just on the feeling or maybe an image. This may be at or away from work, but we suggest a time when you are feeling unwound and calm, yet alert enough to be open to what you need to know.

Transforming the Pain: A Workbook on Vicarious Traumatization
Saakvitne, Pearlman, & Staff of TSI/CAAP (Norton, 1996)

Begin to focus on the feeling or image. Now that you have that image or a sense of that feeling, pick up the colors and express that on paper—maintaining your inward focus, expressing images and feelings with color and form. You may express it in any way you wish, using an image of a tree, a human figure or expression, shapes or images, use of color, or any other expression.

2. For this second part, I'd like you to shift your focus to your feelings, impressions, images, or other aspects of your internal world while with (or just following) clients with whom the impact of your work together is difficult. Remember the imagery, feelings from their stories, what they are struggling with within themselves and in their work with you. Perhaps this is someone with whom it is difficult to feel like you are able to help or have an impact. The imagery may be particularly intrusive, painful, or disturbing. Again, using color and images, reflect these feelings on paper.

3. Now take in a deep breath and exhale. I'd like to remind you of the calm place of the first drawing. Breathe deeply. Now, remembering both the first and second drawings, I invite you to work with the images and color and feelings you expressed in the second drawing. Take some time to begin to see how the experience, the feeling, the drawing can be transformed into an image or experience that would provide additional strength or hope for you in this difficult work. Use colors and images to depict this transformation.

Processing

1. Now, we ask that you form pairs to talk about what you've just done. What has it been like to express your feelings with color and images? Share your observations, awareness, and understanding of feelings elicited by your art. What paths did you

Transforming the Pain: A Workbook on Vicarious Traumatization
Saakvitne, Pearlman, & Staff of TSI/CAAP (Norton, 1996)

discover for transforming painful images and feelings? Try to use a co-listening format, that is, one in which the listener hears the speaker's impressions, images, and thoughts, but does not try to make sense or organize or respond to them. Listen without interpreting, analyzing, helping, or judging. Let go of having to solve any problems. Just listen. Just relax.

2. For anyone who chooses, please share with the larger group any impressions or feelings growing out of this exercise. What have you learned about yourself? To what have you become more open? Is there something from this exercise you can take with you?

Transforming the Pain: A Workbook on Vicarious Traumatization
Saakvitne, Pearlman, & Staff of TSI/CAAP (Norton, 1996)

DRAW-A-TREE SERIES

This second art therapy exercise asks participants to do a series of tree drawings.

First, give participants several sheets of blank paper and an array of drawing utensils. Then ask each person simply to "draw a tree." No further elaboration is needed; allow approximately 5-10 minutes for completion of the drawings.

After participants complete their first drawings, ask them to "draw a comforting tree."

When this drawing is completed, ask them to "draw a wounded tree."

Finally, ask them to "draw a healing tree."

Now, invite everyone to display their drawings, ideally by taping them to a wall or laying them out on a table. Then begin a discussion by asking participants to notice their feelings and the related images elicited by each instruction and to link these feelings to their work as therapists.

The exercise may be concluded with a guided visualization in which each participant is invited to imagine a visit to the tree of his or her choice.

TREES ACROSS THE WORK DAY

In a variation of Draw-a-Tree Series, ask participants to draw a tree that shows how they feel at the beginning of their work day, then a tree that shows how they feel at the end of a work day, and, finally, a tree that shows how they feel at the end of a good therapy session. Again, the pictures should be presented and displayed. Invite the group to discuss their images. For example, ask, "What do the images reveal about the impact of your work or your sense of well-being?" People often note a new awareness of how their work can both deplete and rejuvenate them.

Transforming the Pain: A Workbook on Vicarious Traumatization
Saakvitne, Pearlman, & Staff of TSI/CAAP (Norton, 1996)

Guided Visualizations

A powerful antidote to vicarious traumatization is to discover one's own inner resources for wisdom, soothing, spiritual renewal, and transformation. One route to this discovery is through guided visualizations. A guided visualization involves a brief (5- to 15-minute) directed relaxation exercise followed by a specific series of suggestions for the participants to visualize or imagine. The visualization commonly lasts 10 to 20 minutes; it is followed by a brief return to a relaxed state and then usually processed with some discussion or writing.

Guided visualization is not hypnosis and participants can participate to whatever degree they feel comfortable. For some people, however, experiences such as meditation, relaxation, guided imagery, and guided visualization evoke similar responses to hypnosis, trance induction, and very occasionally a paradoxical response. Any participant can choose to simply listen to the words of the facilitator with eyes open, and just notice what thoughts, ideas, and feelings come to mind.*

The purpose of guided visualization is to practice relaxation skills, improve inner attunement and focus, and increase awareness of inner resources. Some guided visualizations have specific goals as well.

The three guided visualizations presented here have been helpful in vicarious traumatization group work. Commonly people get into comfortable positions, sometimes lying down if there is space, and close their eyes or face away from others in order not to be distracted by external cues. For all guided visualizations, the speaker's voice should be gentle though audible, steady, and warm, but with little expression. In the relaxation section especially, it is important to speak slowly and gently, with long pauses between words and longer pauses between

---

* People who are particularly susceptible to trance states or prefer not to participate may choose to leave the room.

sentences. It is a good idea to read the text completely and to practice reading it aloud before leading a group exercise. Time perception may be altered for participants, so it is important not to move through the exercise too quickly.

These are three examples of more involved experiential exercises, involving relaxation, guided imagery, and focal exercises. Each starts with an introduction and a relaxation component, often followed by some safe place imagery, then a focal task, a transition, and a discussion.

As you practice leading guided visualizations, you will find certain approaches work better for you. Feel free to mix and match among the relaxation, safe place, and transition texts. Often it is useful to have instrumental music as background to a guided visualization. The music is especially helpful if there is significant background noise or distractions.

The first exercise, Befriending Emotion, is given with detailed instructions for each component part: the introduction to the exercise, the relaxation phase, the safe place phase, the focal exercise, the wind down, and the discussion phase. Later examples will include more abbreviated versions of the first phases.

Befriending Emotion* is particularly useful for improving affect tolerance and other self capacities. It helps participants examine their relationship to their own feelings and allows them to see the benefits as well as hardships of particular feelings. Often our fear of strong feelings leads us to employ strong defenses against them (e.g., numbing, denial, avoidance, dissociation), which then create more disconnection and problems. This exercise allows us to face the fears and understand at a deeper level some of the strong feelings evoked by our work.

The second exercise, Future Self, is very popular and very meaningful. It helps participants realize their own inner wisdom and inner

---

*Thanks to Debra Neumann, Ph.D., who developed this exercise after reading John Wellwood's chapter, "Befriending Emotion" (Wellwood, 1983).

resources. After the exercise, participants are often aware of internal strengths and understanding they had not recognized before. Because the resources are within each individual, the exercise reinforces the fact that each person has these resources at all times—even when one feels overwhelmed and helpless.

The third exercise, Conversation and Letters, invites trauma professionals to identify different aspects of themselves that may conflict on issues of self-care. By creating a dialogue between conflicting needs and obligations, participants are invited to examine their underlying beliefs and assess their caretaking strategies. This exercise involves relaxation, guided visualization, and writing, and takes about an hour.

Pearlman and Saakvitne (1995a) state, "The pathognomonic sign of vicarious traumatization is the disruption to the therapist's spirituality" (p. 287). Attending to this spiritual damage is the goal of all vicarious traumatization interventions. Each of these guided visualizations invites the participant to integrate different levels of awareness and self-knowledge. Each offers an opportunity for deeper spiritual awareness and hope for the helper. These exercises are powerful tools whose benefits often outlast the participant's memory of specific content from a workshop.

> In the Future Self exercise, my future self thanked my younger self for taking risks, for doing some rebellious things (like leaving home to go to college out-of-state). She said, "If you hadn't done those things, I wouldn't be who I am now." I felt so validated—by myself.
>
> —*VT workshop participant, a family therapist working with high-risk families.*

BEFRIENDING EMOTION

Introduction

As professionals working in the field of trauma, we are challenged to bear the emotions evoked in us by our clients' material and projections as we help them develop their own tolerance for strong affect. At times, this "holding" contributes to our experience of vicarious traumatization. This exercise will focus on the deepening and acceptance of our own emotions and increase our awareness of the underlying healing energy which is always available to us.

The first step will be to enter into a deeply relaxed state in a safe and grounded space, which you will create by using your own imagery. (Pause)

Then I will ask you to invite a particular emotion, one which you find distressing, to be present with you in this safe space. This emotion may be one that is evoked in your work with clients or a countertransference response to a particular person. It may be a sense of inadequacy or shame, or a more general loss of enjoyment or grief, or an experience of helplessness in what you do. (Pause)

As we sit with our feeling, we will let it speak to us, cutting through our negative judgments about it, and our urge to escape the feeling. We will sit with and befriend the emotion, allowing ourselves to feel it as fully as is comfortable at this time. As we enter this feeling state, we can identify with its energy and let this energy join with our energy, connecting with a shared sense of aliveness made possible by our encounter with this emotion. (Pause)

Now we will take leave of this particular feeling, and after resting a short while in our safe and grounded place, we will return to a fully alert state.

Transforming the Pain: A Workbook on Vicarious Traumatization
Saakvitne, Pearlman, & Staff of TSI/CAAP (Norton, 1996)

Relaxation

I would now like each of you to close your eyes gently. Make yourself comfortable in your chair. You may want to relax your body into the seat, letting your arms lie loosely at your side, or in your lap. Listen carefully to my voice as you focus on your breathing. In and out. In and out. With each breath in you feel more relaxed and peaceful. As you release your breath, tension flows out with it. In and out. In and out. Sink deeper into a relaxed state, being comfortably aware of your body relaxing in your chair, listening to my voice as it goes on, and your breath going in and out. As you listen quietly to my voice, your breathing is deepening, and you are taking slow, deep, gentle breaths, letting the air go all the way down into your abdomen. As you breathe in slowly and deeply, continue to notice that with each breath in you are feeling more and more relaxed and comfortable, and with each breath out any tension you might have been holding gently leaves your body.

In and out. In and out. Let each muscle in your body relax completely, relaxing more and more as your breathing becomes slower and deeper. Let the relaxed sensation spread from the muscles in the top of your head, down through the muscles in your face, and neck, and into your shoulders, now spreading down through your arms and upper body. And as the relaxation spreads throughout your body, you feel it pushing all the tension and strain away from you, down through your arms and hands and fingers and out into the air, far, far away from you. You may feel a warm, glowing sensation inside.

As you continue to breathe in and out now, you are aware of the wave of relaxation spreading throughout your whole body. Down through your torso and into your legs . . . the wave is pushing any remaining tension ahead of this relaxed feeling, down through your legs, and feet and toes, and out away from you. All the tension

Transforming the Pain: A Workbook on Vicarious Traumatization
Saakvitne, Pearlman, & Staff of TSI/CAAP (Norton, 1996)

floats away, far from where you are now. And you feel good all over, comfortable and grounded and relaxed. Notice how the relaxed sensation moves along with your breath. In and out. In and out. Relaxed and resting. And should you at any time begin to feel tense or anxious, you will be able to notice your breathing, this reliable in and out, and you will be able to reconnect with this grounded and relaxed feeling.

Safe Place

Now imagine that you are in a very pleasant and protected place. This may be a place you have been before, perhaps a time you spent at the ocean, in the mountains, a lake, or a special room, or it may be a place you've imagined before or for the first time. Whatever you imagine, it is a very comfortable, safe, and pleasing place for you to be. In your mind's eye, you can vividly see yourself there now, and you can sense that all around you are the colors and sounds and smells of this lovely and safe place. Take some time now just to enjoy being in this place as you continue to breathe in and out, in and out, feeling relaxed and grounded and comfortable, supported by your breathing, feeling a complete sense of well-being. All fear is gone, because you can always return to this pleasant protected place you've imagined and focus on your gentle breathing to stay relaxed and comfortable.

Focal Exercise

As you are resting in this quiet place, a situation from your clinical or professional work will come to mind. This may be a situation in which you experienced some distressing emotion, one that is difficult for you to bear, or an ongoing experience of difficulty with your work. As the emotion comes to mind, allow yourself to approach it a bit, or you may want to invite it to come toward you.

Transforming the Pain: A Workbook on Vicarious Traumatization
Saakvitne, Pearlman, & Staff of TSI/CAAP (Norton, 1996)

Keep an awareness of your breathing, in and out, and of your safe and pleasant place, your support, and your grounding. As the distressing emotion comes closer, you may wish to give it a form, perhaps resembling a gremlin of some sort or a type of animal. Or maybe it is more like something from nature, like a dark heavy cloud or thunder. Sit with this emotion for a moment and notice what it looks like and how it feels to be with it. Without judging or resisting it, just allow yourself to experience the feeling, always being aware of your breathing, in and out, in and out.

Now you may feel ready to approach the emotion even more closely, if you choose. And you may find that the feeling has something to tell you, something about yourself or your client that will be helpful to you. Listen to it. Perhaps you have something to say to this feeling as well. Let yourself enter the feeling, as you breathe in and out, staying aware of your grounding. Let yourself notice how you feel as you sit with this emotion. Notice the sensations in your body. You will notice the energy contained in the emotion and how, as you move into it, you too are able to connect with this energy and this basic aliveness. Let this feeling of aliveness flow through you, and focus on it as you sit with the emotion and continue to breathe in and out, in and out. Feel your aliveness, your support and groundedness. In and out. (Pause)

Wind Down

Soon it will be time to take leave of the emotion for now. You may say goodbye in whatever way seems best for you, taking your time and letting yourself rest in your comfortable, safe, and pleasant place, feeling relaxed, grounded, and content with your encounter. Rest here a bit, and when you are ready take your time and return to your alert waking self.

Transforming the Pain: A Workbook on Vicarious Traumatization
Saakvitne, Pearlman, & Staff of TSI/CAAP (Norton, 1996)

Discussion

For discussion after this guided visualization exercise, you might ask,

- Would anyone like to share what she or he noticed?
- What emotion did you encounter?
- What form did it take?
- What was it like to be with this emotion in that form?
- How did you approach it?
- What message did you get from it?
- Did you have a message to give to it?

FUTURE SELF

Introduction

This exercise is a combination relaxation / meditation / guided imagery exercise. As part of it, you will visit your future professional self to see what wisdom you can gain from him or her. The exercise will take about 15 minutes, and then we will spend some time talking informally about your experience with the exercise and how it relates to the concept of VT.

Of course, your participation is completely voluntary. I ask however, that once the exercise has begun, you remain quiet and still so others are not distracted.

Relaxation

First, I want to invite you to get as comfortable as possible, in your chair, or using the floor. Take off your shoes if you like, close your eyes if you wish. As you become comfortable, focus on your breathing. As you notice the gentle rhythm of your breath, in and out, in and out, you will feel gentle waves of relaxation envelop you. Tension flows out with every breath out and relaxation flows in with every breath in. You will feel relaxation in every part of your body, from the top of your head, your forehead, eyes, mouth, face, neck, shoulders, arms, hands, torso, pelvis, hips, legs, feet, and toes. All of your body is relaxed and relaxes more with each breath.

Feel yourself floating on a soft and comfortable cloud. Feel the soft air, gentle breeze, and notice you are calm and safe. You may become aware of sounds or thoughts as you breathe. Just allow them to pass and return your attention to your breathing.

Slowly, this cloud will drift, as you wish it, toward the future. Slowly, as you are ready, the cloud will settle and gently disperse, leaving you ready to visit with your future professional self.

Focal Exercise

Imagine entering your future self's office or workspace. As your future self welcomes you, look around. What do you notice about the space? What objects do you see? What do you notice about your future self? What do you look like? How have you changed, grown, and matured? Take some time and notice the feelings you have in the room. Breathe in the air, and take the opportunity now to find a place to sit opposite or beside your future self. Feel your body supported in the seat you have chosen. Notice the temperature in the room. Look at the light and colors, notice any smells.

Listen now as you and your future self converse about your work-life. Are there any questions you wish to ask your future self? Go ahead and ask those now . . . and listen to your future self's thoughtful response. How does your future self feel about the work? What is most rewarding? What are some proudest memories? What is most comforting? (Pause)

How does your future self feel at the end of a day of work? Listen and ask any questions that come to mind. (Pause)

Is there anything your future self would like to ask you? Anything she or he wants to tell or suggest to you, or to give to you? (Pause)

Although only a short amount of clock time has elapsed, you can sense that you have had all the time you need for now with your future self. Your time together is almost complete and your future self invites you to bring back with you anything you wish. Is there something in the office, some aspect or object, that will help you remain connected to your future self? You may pick it out and take it back to the present with you. (Pause)

It is time to say goodbye. You know you will meet at some future point.

Transforming the Pain: A Workbook on Vicarious Traumatization
Saakvitne, Pearlman, & Staff of TSI/CAAP (Norton, 1996)

Wind Down

As you close the door, let the soft cloud pick you up and drift at a comfortable pace back toward the present. Let yourself slowly return to this room, feeling you have had all the time you need. As I count from 10 to 1, you'll feel progressively more and more alert and present. (Count from 10 to 1, intermittently reminding people that they are returning to the present, alert and rested, and will shortly be ready to open their eyes.) Gently return to your body in the present and open your eyes as you are ready.

Discussion

In the discussion that follows the guided visualization, some of the questions you might address are:

- What did your future self and future space look like?

- How did she or he respond to feelings?

- What did you learn from her or him? What did you take with you?

- What was it like to see yourself in the future?

- What changes did you notice?

This exercise can also be done asking people to visit a wise woman (or man, or person); this wise one can be someone they have known in their life or the wise part of themselves.

Transforming the Pain: A Workbook on Vicarious Traumatization
Saakvitne, Pearlman, & Staff of TSI/CAAP (Norton, 1996)

CONVERSATION AND LETTERS

Relaxation

I'd like to invite you to make yourself comfortable, to unwind and untangle your arms and legs, to find a position in which you can relax comfortably.

When you find the position that is comfortable for you, I'd like to suggest that you slow down your mind in order to pay attention to your breathing. Just notice your breathing. As you begin to focus on your breathing, you may wish to slow it down, to begin to take some slow, deep, gentle breaths.

And you might begin to notice that as your breathing begins to slow, as you begin to take slow, deep, gentle breaths, each time you inhale you take in calm, refreshing air, and each time you exhale you release some tension. Inhale, taking in calm, clean air. Exhale, letting go of tension. As you continue to take slow, deep, gentle breaths, you might take the time to notice any remaining areas of tension in your body. You might want to gather up that tension as you inhale, then release it with the air that you exhale.

You might want to concentrate on what I say, or you might allow your mind to wander and find its own path, with the sound of my voice in the background. Do not be concerned if my voice becomes the background for your own reverie; when I wish to call your attention to instructions for the writing exercise, I will suggest that it is time to return from your reverie to the meaning of my words, and you will easily be able to shift.

Safe Place

We will think in a few moments about the stresses and rewards of our work, but for a moment we will allow our minds to wander, perhaps to a special place, far away from the pressures and strong

Transforming the Pain: A Workbook on Vicarious Traumatization
Saakvitne, Pearlman, & Staff of TSI/CAAP (Norton, 1996)

feelings at work—a beautiful place, perhaps somewhere you have been or maybe a place you visit only in your mind, safe from pressures or intense feelings.

Walk around or simply notice this space. What do you see? Notice the colors, their intensity or their mutedness. What shapes do you see? Do you see a beautiful landscape or seascape? What objects do you observe? Is there light? Shade? What can you feel? Warm or cool, soft or hard sensations? What textures? What can you touch? What smells or sounds are you aware of?

Find a spot, in your special secluded place, to sit and rest a while, where you can think about your own particular reactions to this work. (Pause)

Conversation

It is time to return from your reverie to the meaning of my words. You will notice your attention being drawn to the meaning of my words, and although you can remain pleasantly relaxed you will be alert to what I am saying.

Working with the pain of others, particularly the pain of people who have been traumatized, leaves all of us vulnerable. There are many ways that we increase our own vulnerability.

We might rush heedlessly into stressful situations, then wonder why we feel overwhelmed. We might take on clients without thoughtful consideration of the ways our own issues interact with theirs, then wonder why we feel besieged. We might take responsibility for things we can't control, then wonder why we feel out of control. We might ignore the warning signs our bodies send us, then wonder why we get sick, develop back problems, overeat, or feel lethargic.

Transforming the Pain: A Workbook on Vicarious Traumatization
Saakvitne, Pearlman, & Staff of TSI/CAAP (Norton, 1996)

I invite you to think about the ways that you leave yourself vulnerable to even greater stress than the work normally entails. How do you neglect to protect yourself? (Pause)

Some of us put no limits on our availability, thus overloading ourselves and failing to help our clients learn to cope on their own. Some of us ignore our own issues, neglecting the need for our own therapy. Some of us never really take a break, filling our spare time with technical reading and working, neglecting our need for a life outside of and apart from our work.

I'd like you to identify one way that you leave yourself more vulnerable to stress than necessary. Think about how you do that. Notice the part of yourself that is particularly vulnerable to doing this. You might find that it begins to be possible to identify the part of yourself that makes these choices without blaming or shaming yourself.

I'm going to pause for a moment so that in the quiet, you can allow these ideas to take shape in your mind. In the quiet, you can begin to discover that part of yourself that is leaving you more vulnerable to stress than necessary. (Pause)

Next I'd like to turn your attention again to that faraway place, far away from the pressures and emotions of work, where you can once again feel some distance from the stress and from your own vulnerabilities to stress. I'm going to invite you to discover another aspect of your self: a wise, nurturing, caring, loving part of yourself. This part knows that the work we do means bearing witness to atrocity, holding the pain of others, and becoming an unwilling participant in traumatic reenactments. This part of us offers nurturing and caring to clients who are often unable to respond, without giving up on them. Inside of you, there is a part of yourself, an inner core, with a great capacity for caring, for giving, for

Transforming the Pain: A Workbook on Vicarious Traumatization
Saakvitne, Pearlman, & Staff of TSI/CAAP (Norton, 1996)

nurturing people through the healing process. There is also wisdom, gathered through life experience, everything our clients teach us, and all we have learned, that we can draw upon to support *ourselves* in this work.

As we linger for a while in this special, beautiful, secluded place, I'd like to invite you to identify and sit with this wise, nurturing aspect of yourself. Inside of you, in this part of yourself, you can find whatever you need to know to support yourself in this work and help yourself through vicarious traumatization.

And as you identify and remain with this aspect of your self, your inner core, listen quietly for the wisdom inside of you. (Pause)

Letters: Writing to Oneself

In a few minutes, we'll ask this part of yourself to write, to write a letter to that part of you that is so vulnerable to the stress involved in this work. You won't have to work hard to write this letter because the wise, nurturing part of you already knows what you need to take better care of yourself. This part of you is skilled in taking care and knows what you need to know about your own vulnerabilities to the pain and pressure of this work.

Let us take a moment to use that great skill in caretaking for someone very deserving—yourself. We will pause for a moment, and after the pause, you can take up your pen and paper and write that letter to the part of yourself who needs this type of care. (Pause)

[Participants write letters.]

When you are done, fold and put the letter aside. Let's talk for a few minutes about the exercise. I invite people to discuss and share any parts of their experience that feel okay to be public. How do you leave yourself vulnerable to the stress of this work? How does your wise inner core recommend you address this?

I'm going to ask you to write again. This time, briefly summarize the main points, how you leave yourself vulnerable, and what your wise self knows you need for protection.

Put the first letter in the envelope provided, seal it, and address it to yourself. I will mail this to you in 2 months. I suggest you hold onto the second list and use it as a reminder of what you've learned here today.

Transforming the Pain: A Workbook on Vicarious Traumatization
Saakvitne, Pearlman, & Staff of TSI/CAAP (Norton, 1996)

Chapter 5
Maintaining the Commitment

I recently identified that I need a break, but now I would say that I am suffering from VT. This workshop could not have come at a better time for me. My feelings were validated and it brought some clarity to the blizzard I have felt buried in. Now I just need to determine if I need more time off or to return to work. I think I'll return—now I have the tools!

—*VT workshop participant, an aide at a residential program for chemically dependent adolescents*

Now we must address the pivotal question: How do we make a commitment to ourselves to address vicarious traumatization *and* sustain that commitment over time? To identify vicarious traumatization is not terribly difficult; in any given moment most of us can fairly readily agree to pay better attention to our needs and take more self-protective steps. But it is extraordinarily difficult for each of us to maintain that commitment over time.

What Helps Us Maintain Our Commitment?

Taking it Seriously

Those in emergency and helping professions take commitments seriously and follow through on them, especially commitments made to others. Now we must extend that commitment to ourselves. Vicarious

---

Making a Personal Commitment to Oneself and One's Work

Why?

- Because I hurt
- Because I matter
- Because my clients matter
- Because the work I do matters
- Because the profession matters
- Because I must

How?

- Not alone; get a buddy or a group
- One day at a time
- Do something in each realm
- One change at a time
- Increase mindfulness and acceptance
- Don't forget and don't give up

---

traumatization profoundly affects the quality of our lives. For that reason alone, it is important to address it. *We matter*. In addition, vicarious traumatization also affects the quality of our work, and therefore our clients' experience. Ultimately it affects the reputation and well-being of our professions. Thus, we have a responsibility to ourselves, our friends, partners, and families, as well as our clients and our professions to address vicarious traumatization.

Being Realistic

None of us can maintain the commitment all alone. We need support from our colleagues, organizations, friends, partners, and families. If you do not already have a support network for addressing vicarious traumatization, we recommend that you get yourself a buddy or a group of colleagues who will join you in making a commitment to addressing vicarious traumatization. Make sure you have contact with your buddy or group members weekly—at a minimum.

If your partner, family, or friends don't "get it," consider showing them the videotapes on vicarious traumatization (listed in the annotated bibliography). Have a discussion with them about how you can protect yourself—and them—from the negative impact of your work.

If your organization doesn't recognize vicarious traumatization, start with education. Have readings on vicarious traumatization and available for all staff members. Show the videotapes at a staff meeting and begin a discussion on organizational strategies to address vicarious traumatization. Make the point with administrators that it is cost-effective to address vicarious traumatization for several reasons:

1. Vicarious traumatization can lead to poor clinical work, especially lack of follow-through, boundary violations, and poor judgment. Professional errors cost the organization and the profession in terms of lost referrals, negative public image, complaints, and lawsuits.

2. Vicarious traumatization leads to absenteeism and high staff turnover, resulting in a less experienced, less cohesive, and less effective staff. Not only are hiring and training enormously expensive ventures, but the quality of the service offered by the organization will suffer as a result.

3. Staff members who are protecting themselves from vicarious traumatization and are exercising good self-care and hope-

sustaining behaviors are likely to be motivated, open to new learning, and doing their jobs well. The best advertisement for any service organization is satisfied customers, clients, and referral sources.

4. Addressing vicarious traumatization does not have to be an expensive venture. Using one meeting a week, providing reasonable work expectations and a reasonable amount of self-determination (e.g., choices about client balance and scheduling) for professional staff are achievable tasks for most organizations.

What Gets in the Way?

In the Professional Realm

At work we always encounter obstacles to self-care. We often carry misguided assumptions about our own invulnerability and mistakenly equate stoicism with professionalism. There are endless demands on our time and energy; there are countless opportunities to skip lunch, take another client, return six phone calls, help someone else out, and ignore our physical, emotional, and psychic selves. In the short run our clients, colleagues, and administrators feel they benefit from our overextension; therefore we must be the guardians of our boundaries and limits for our own and, ultimately, their long-term well-being.

By creating a schedule that builds sanity and self-care into each day, we protect ourselves and those we serve. Wherever possible, make decisions ahead of time about availability, nourishment, and pacing. In the moment, too frequently we are persuaded to abandon ourselves in the service of someone else. Plan a schedule of direct client contact, meetings, supervision, and other professional obligations that includes breaks for exercise, rest, and nourishment. Plan a weekly and monthly

Sample Clinical Schedules

A. Several short breaks

9:00 – 9:50	client
10:00 –10:50	client
10:50 –11:15	mail, phone calls
11:15 –12:05	supervision
12:05 –12:30	lunch
12:30 – 1:20	client
1:30 – 2:20	client
2:30 – 3:20	administrative meeting
3:20 – 3:45	break
3:45 – 4:35	client
4:45 – 5:35	client

B. One large break midday

7:00 – 7:50	client
8:00 – 8:50	client
8:50 – 9:10	coffee and mail
9:10 –10:00	supervision
10:00 – 1:00	PERSONAL TIME
1:00 – 1:50	client
2:00 – 2:50	client
3:00 – 3:50	meeting
3:50 – 4:15	phone calls, stretching
4:15 – 5:05	client

schedule that allows for continuing education, variation of tasks, and time off. Even five minutes of focused relaxation can make an enormous difference in our ability to remain grounded and self-connected.

Write out your weekly schedule on a blank sheet of paper. Examine it with an eye to what it says about your self-expectations. Does your schedule reflect an expectation that you are tireless, without needs? Does it reflect attention to pacing and self-care? Is it humane—or punishing? Above are two sample clinical schedules for a full-time employee.

In the Organizational Realm

Organizations can unwittingly create a climate that is at worst hostile or at best antithetical to self-care. When an organization serving trauma survivors focuses solely on revenue, to the exclusion of quality of care for its clients and quality of life for its employees, it supports vicarious traumatization. There are many social and economic pressures on social services. Too often administrators are drawn into reactive, short-term, solution-focused approaches that ignore the larger picture and the long-term effects of expeditious decisions. It takes a talented administrator to balance the need for economic survival with the need for reasonable standards for the direct service staff. Administrators often have other sources of vicarious traumatization as they try to balance the demands and anxieties of their work. They also need to pay special attention to their own vicarious traumatization.

Organizations need to be educated and members of the organization need to take initiative. Making time for supervision, direct or peer, requires everyone's cooperation. Creating meeting time to process or simply speak about the impact of our work is powerful and helpful and requires group participation. At TSI/CAAP, we use 40 to 50 minutes of our weekly case conference for "feelings time," an opportunity to talk about our feelings about the work we do and its impact on us. During that time, we cannot be disturbed; the meeting is protected and private in the same way our therapy sessions with clients are protected from interruption or intrusion. As therapists, we use the time to discuss countertransference, vicarious traumatization, and responses to systemic and societal factors in our work.

In the Personal Realm

Outside of work, we are subject to other demands. Our day-to-day lives require attention. Trauma treaters who have children have endless demands for their time, attention, and caregiving. Pet owners have responsibilities to their animals. Homeowners have the demands of the care and upkeep of their homes. Most of us have health care concerns, bills, student loans, and maintenance tasks that demand our money, time, and attention. We all have friends and family who need us and want our time.

When we work long hours, bring our work home, or have work intrusions (like crisis phone calls) into our home life, our partners and families will sometimes be resentful and intolerant of our work-related needs. Their frustration will be harder to negotiate if they do not understand the nature of our work or its profound impact on us as individuals.

Again, planning ahead to create time and space for healing activities, both alone and with others, minimizes the struggle. *Transition* time from work to home is especially important. It is helpful to develop a brief ritual for leaving the office that allows you to leave the day's material behind. This may include drawing or writing something for yourself that represents what you wish to leave behind for the day, arranging your office in a way that will feel welcoming tomorrow, or even simply sitting quietly for a few moments and meditating. Use your commute—drive, walk, bus, or subway—to relax and shift gears: for some that means soothing music; for others, raucous music; for others, books-on-tape or news; and for some it means silence. Notice your body as you travel. Notice your breathing and consciously slow it down and deepen it.

When you get home, identify a transition strategy for you. It might be to change your clothes or take a shower or bath. It may be sitting still and silent for ten minutes, or talking with your partner about your respective days, but with a time limit on work topics. It may mean creating a bubble of silence around you for a set period of time that people in your home can learn to expect and respect after which you will be available to talk and connect with them. Notice what *you* need to allow yourself to transition and so be fully present for your time at home, by yourself, or with others.

In all realms the major danger is that we could ignore or again become unaware of the impact of our work and of our defenses against the feelings it evokes. It is easy to become numb or superficially active and remain unaware that we are avoiding connection with ourselves and those we love. Maintaining our awareness in all realms is the first and hardest step to maintaining our commitment.

What's at Stake: The Cost of Failing Yourself

We have described the far-reaching effects of vicarious traumatization. It harms the helper, the helper's family and loved ones, the helper's clients and colleagues, and the profession and the larger society. When we accept VT as a normal and predictable response we can be free to identify ameliorative strategies and to provide support for ourselves, our colleagues, and students.

Vicarious Traumatization and Hope

We cannot continue to do the work we do or to survive as a people or a society without hope. Yet, we cannot be repeatedly exposed to trauma without building up defenses against the pain and sorrow of our work. Cynicism and indifference are two lethal byproducts of vicarious traumatization. Therefore, unless we address our vicarious traumatization, we are going to close our hearts and minds to that which sustains us in our work and in our lives. We cannot afford to ignore vicarious traumatization or to abandon hope at any level—personal, professional, or societal. Understanding vicarious traumatization then is essential to sustaining hope.

The Rewards of Our Work

One of the things that sustains us and counteracts vicarious traumatization is the hope we gain from our work. Working with trauma survivors brings remarkable rewards. Trauma survivors get better. They heal and grow and find their voices to speak out against abuse and injustice. Witnessing pain brings with it the possibility of witnessing healing. The impact of trauma is modifiable; traumatic stress is treatable. Humans who survive trauma have great inner strengths and wisdom that can be used on their own behalf.

Through our work, we also witness the resilience of the human spirit and the remarkable resourcefulness of the human mind. Humans' capacity for love, kindness, and generosity is as real as the human capacity for cruelty and selfishness. Heroism is as real as villainy.

None of us works alone. There are many of us, each adding our thread to the tapestry of healing. We know far more now than we did five or twenty years ago, and we will continue weaving together our experiences to increase the knowledge about healing from trauma.

The concept of vicarious traumatization is a new development. By understanding the effect of the work on the helper, we move the field of traumatic stress forward; we are able to work more effectively toward our shared goals.

Models for Vicarious Traumatization Interventions

To sustain your commitment to addressing vicarious traumatization on an ongoing basis, you need support. There are several possible ways to structure that support.

Individual and Pair Approaches

In an individual or pair approach, each person makes an individual commitment and tailors strategies to meet his or her unique needs. While many strategies can be implemented individually, collaboration with a colleague can strengthen the commitment and, for some strategies, the benefits. Pairs of individuals, or buddies, can make a commitment to one another to meet regularly and discuss feelings evoked by the work, and perhaps to try some of the restorative exercises described in the previous chapter or available in books on the resource list.

When two meet for such a purpose, they can agree to use a peer model in which both participants share the time equally. Alternatively, vicarious traumatization work can be integrated into ongoing supervision (see chapter 17 in Pearlman & Saakvitne, 1995a), or a vicarious traumatization consultation can be set up with one person presenting and the other responding.

Vicarious Traumatization Groups

A group formed to address vicarious traumatization can create a structure that helps each member maintain his or her personal commitment. Vicarious traumatization groups can adopt different formats. A weekly staff meeting, for example, can be used to address the experience of trauma workers and the impact of the work on them. This model has the advantage of involving available colleagues in the process of acknowledging and addressing vicarious traumatization. It can create an active support network at the workplace. On the other hand, some professionals may feel that this degree of intimacy or vulnerability is inappropriate or imprudent with immediate colleagues, especially if they have very different orientations or direct supervisory or administrative authority over the individual. In any case, confidentiality and expectations for the group must be clear. For example, there should be explicit acknowledgment that expressions of feelings are not signs of weakness or incompetence, and that the purpose of the meeting is to address the normal and inevitable feelings aroused by the work, otherwise shame and fear will preclude open and effective processing.

A group at the Boston Veterans' Administration Hospital has developed a team model for preventing compassion fatigue (Munroe, et al., 1995). Describing an outpatient intensive treatment program for combat veterans, they posit that "the most effective place for a preventative community is the work site where secondary traumatization takes place" (p. 212). Their treatment team operates on three primary assumptions: "(1) no therapist is immune to the effects of secondary trauma, (2) prevention of secondary trauma lies in the membership of a team, and (3) the higher the intensity of exposure to trauma work, the greater is the need for a team" (p. 227). Within this team,

> Team members regularly pose questions about secondary traumatization that include: (1) How are team members being engaged? (2) How do they feel about it? (3) What will we do about it? Therapist self-care is expected, and the team reminds members of this if they neglect this responsibility. . . . Overwork is discouraged. The feelings of team members are considered important. (p. 228)

This model is described in more detail in a chapter in *Compassion Fatigue* (Figley, 1995). This edited volume has several helpful chapters that offer ways to identify and address the impact of work with trauma survivors on treaters.

Another model for a vicarious traumatization group is described by Guzzino and Taxis (1995), an experiential group with two therapist facilitators that meets for three hours every month. In this group, the leaders decide the membership criteria and decide whether colleagues working together can be in the same group. The leaders take an active role in structuring the work of the group and addressing the specific needs of the individual participants.

A regular supervision group can agree to focus some of their meetings on vicarious traumatization issues, both in discussion and in specific assessment and intervention techniques. Alternatively, a group may form with the explicit wish to be a peer vicarious traumatization group. The group can alternate general discussion of members' concerns and experiences with exercises. Group members can rotate responsibility for leading different exercises and the discussion that follows them.

Another option is for staff members or colleagues to set time aside periodically for an in-depth intervention; for example, at TSI/CAAP we set aside 1 to 1½ hours at each of our biannual retreats for a vicarious traumatization exercise and discussion. Staff may hire a psychodramatist or art therapist to do a group intervention on an occasional basis.

People can also attend intensive workshops or conferences specifically addressing vicarious traumatization and therapist self-care. These workshops may be anywhere from a half-day to a week in length. They often interweave didactic with experiential work to help attendees integrate the material and develop a personal understanding and assessment of their own experience of vicarious traumatization.

Identifying Next Steps

What was helpful? The challenge to become aware and then to act.
> —*VT workshop participant, a psychiatrist in private practice who also consults to a battered women's shelter*

As you finish this workbook, ask yourself: What are my next steps? In each realm of my life, what can I do next to start or continue my commitment to remain aware and attentive to the ongoing impact of my work on my health and well-being? Use the worksheet on the next page to identify your next steps. To maintain your commitment to yourself, we suggest that you return to this worksheet regularly.

Next Steps

In my personal life my next step is:

In my professional life my next step is:

In my organization my next step is:

I am making a commitment to myself to take steps.

Transforming the Pain: A Workbook on Vicarious Traumatization
Saakvitne, Pearlman, & Staff of TSI/CAAP (Norton, 1996)

References

Davies, J. M., & Frawley, M. G. (1994). *Treating the adult survivor of childhood sexual abuse: A psychoanalytic perspective.* New York: Basic.

* Figley, C. R. (Ed.). (1995). *Compassion fatigue: Coping with secondary traumatic stress disorder in those who treat the traumatized.* New York: Brunner/Mazel.

Frankl, V. (1959). *Man's search for meaning: An introduction to logotherapy.* New York: Washington Square Press.

Freud, S. (1910). The Future Prospects of Psychoanalytic Therapy. In J. Strachey (Ed. and Trans.), *The standard edition of the complete psychological works of Sigmund Freud* (Vol. 11, pp. 139–151). New York: Norton.

Gamble, S. J., Pearlman, L. A., Lucca, A. M., Allen, G. J. (1994, October 29). *Vicarious traumatization and burnout in Connecticut psychologists: Empirical findings.* Paper presented at the Annual Meeting of the Connecticut Psychological Association, Waterbury, CT.

* Guzzino, M. H., & Taxis, C. (1995). Leading experiential vicarious trauma groups for professionals. *Treating Abuse Today, 4*(1), 27–31.

* Hahn, T. N. (1976). *The miracle of mindfulness: A manual on meditation.* Boston: Beacon.

---

* Also listed in annotated bibliography.

Kabat–Zinn, J. (1994). *Wherever you go, there you are: Mindfulness meditation in everyday life.* New York: Hyperion.

Linehan, M. (1993a). *Cognitive behavioral treatment of borderline personality disorder.* New York: Guilford.

* Linehan, M. (1993b). *Skills training manual for treating borderline personality disorder.* New York: Guilford.

Maltz, W. (1992). Caution: Treating sexual abuse can be hazardous to your love life. *Treating Abuse Today, 2*(2), 20–24.

McCann, I. L., & Pearlman, L. A. (1990a). Vicarious traumatization: A framework for understanding the psychological effects of working with victims. *Journal of Traumatic Stress, 3*(1), 131–149.

* McCann, I. L., & Pearlman, L. A. (1990b). *Psychological trauma and the adult survivor: Theory, therapy, and transformation.* New York: Brunner/Mazel.

Miller, D. (1994). *Women who hurt themselves: A book of hope and understanding.* New York: Basic.

Munroe, J. F., Shay, J., Fisher, L., Makary, C., Rapperport, K., & Zimering, R. (1995). Preventing compassion fatigue: A team treatment model. In C. R. Figley (Ed.), *Compassion fatigue: Coping with secondary traumatic stress disorder in those who treat the traumatized* (pp. 209–231). New York: Brunner/Mazel.

Neumann, D. A. & Gamble, S. J. (1995, Summer) Vicarious traumatization in the new trauma therapist. *Psychotherapy, 32*(2), 341–347.

Neumann, D. A., & Pearlman, L. A. (in press). Review of the Life Orientation Inventory. In B. H. Stamm (Ed.), *Measurement of stress, trauma, and adaptation.* Lutherville, MD: Sidran.

* O'Hara, V. (1995) *Wellness at work: Building resilience to job stress.* Oakland, CA: New Harbinger.

Pearlman, L. A. (in press). Review of the TSI Belief Scale, Revision L. In B. H. Stamm (Ed.), *Measurement of stress, trauma, and adaptation.* Lutherville, MD: Sidran.

Pearlman, L. A., & Mac Ian, P. S. (1995). Vicarious traumatization: An empirical study of the effects of trauma work on trauma therapists. *Professional Psychology, 26*(6), 558–565.

* Pearlman, L. A., & Saakvitne, K. W. (1995a). *Trauma and the therapist: Countertransference and vicarious traumatization in psychotherapy with incest survivors.* New York: Norton.

Pearlman, L. A. & Saakvitne, K. W. (1995b). Treating therapists with vicarious traumatization and secondary traumatic stress disorders. In C. R. Figley (Ed.), *Compassion fatigue: Coping with secondary traumatic stress disorder in those who treat the traumatized* (pp. 150–177). New York: Brunner/Mazel.

*Stamm, B. H. (Ed.). (1995). *Secondary traumatic stress: Self-care issues for clinicians, researchers, and educators.* Lutherville, MD: Sidran.

Wellwood, J. (1983). Befriending emotion. In J. Wellwood (Ed.), *Awakening the heart: East/West approaches to psychotherapy* (pp. 79–90). Boulder, CO: Shambhala.

Annotated Bibliography

Care of the Soul by Thomas Moore (HarperPerennial, 1994)
A classic that opens the reader to consider the sacredness of everyday life. Wordy in places but worth getting through, especially the chapter on "the gifts of depression."

Compassion Fatigue: Coping with Secondary Traumatic Stress Disorder in Those Who Treat the Traumatized edited by Charles R. Figley, Ph.D. (Brunner/Mazel, 1995)
A very useful volume containing chapters on different aspects of vicarious traumatization and secondary traumatic stress disorders in psychotherapy with different populations of trauma survivors.

Dance of the Spirit: The Seven Steps of Women's Spirituality by Maria Harris (Bantam Books, 1991)
Definitely not for women only, this readable book explores spirituality in the broadest sense. Exercises at the end of each chapter promote self-awareness and spiritual self-care.

Drawing from Within: A Workbook for Self-expression and Self-discovery by Barbara Prochelo (SunDance Creations, 1990)
Wonderful drawing exercises help you explore identity, feelings, life themes, and core beliefs. All exercises can be easily adapted for VT interventions.

Finding Joy: 101 Ways to Free Your Spirit and Dance with Life by Charlotte Davis Kasl (HarperPerennial, 1994)

A deceptively simple book that reminds one to be gentle and self-affirming. A pleasure to read. Full of pearls such as, "If someone is throwing garbage out of the window, move!" and "Remember, you get to make mistakes" and "A belief is a belief is a belief . . . but it's not necessarily so."

Full Catastrophe Living: Using the Wisdom of Your Body and Mind to Face Stress, Pain, and Illness by John Kabat-Zinn (Dell, 1990)

A readable and practical book that will be helpful to both novices and old hands at meditation and mindfulness. It discusses the impact of mindfulness and meditation on an individual's general health and well-being as well as their specific use for physical pain and illness.

Healing Into Life and Death by Stephen Levine (Doubleday, 1987)

An extraordinarily wise book that offers meditations to develop "merciful awareness" and a healing attitude of loving kindness toward oneself and the world at large. This work was written to address issues of illness, grief, and loss, and reading any part of this book will be a powerful anti-VT experience.

Healing with the Mind's Eye: A Guide for Using Imagery and Visions for Personal Growth and Healing by Michael and Nancy Samuels (Summit, 1990).

Focusing on the healing power of imagery for both mind and body, the authors offer numerous guided imagery and visualization narratives that can be incorporated as anti-VT practices. Of particular note are the instructions for individuals unaccustomed to using guided imagery.

"Leading Experiential Vicarious Trauma Groups for Professionals" by
M. H. Guzzino & C. Taxis (in *Treating Abuse Today,* 4(1),
27–31, 1995)
 An interesting discussion of a model for a vicarious trauma
group run by an art therapist and a psychodramatist. Discusses
use of creative arts techniques in group building and the working
through of vicarious trauma in a group of therapists.

The Miracle of Mindfulness: A Manual on Meditation by Thich Nhat
Hanh (Beacon, 1976)
 A basic text on mindfulness and meditation skills written by a
Zen teacher. A classic: simple and accessible.

Psychological Trauma and the Adult Survivor by Lisa McCann and
Laurie Anne Pearlman (Brunner/Mazel, 1990)
 A theoretical framework for understanding and treating adult
survivors of traumatic life events. Integrates social, cognitive, and
contemporary psychodynamic theories to guide clinicians in their
work. An excellent textbook as well as a resource for all clinicians. It also provides a helpful framework for survivors.

Pure and Simple Stretch, a video by Karen Voight (Fitness Arts Dis-
tributors [1-800-735-3315], 1991)
 Do this relaxing 35-minute stretching program several times a
week and help your body de-stress. Especially good for those
who tend to get back, neck, and shoulder pain from too much sitting and listening.

Random Acts of Kindness, Books I & II by the Editors of Conari Press
(1993)
 These small books contain many stories of random acts of
kindness, small and large gestures of compassion and generosity
that made a difference. They help a trauma professional remem-

ber that good things happen as well as bad things, and specifically that people can also be humane, generous, loving, and self-
sacrificing. These stories renew faith in humanity and love.

*Secondary Traumatic Stress: Self Care Issues for Clinicians, Re-
searchers, and Educators* edited by Beth Hudnall Stamm (Sidran,
1995)

This excellent small volume includes chapters on secondary
traumatic stress and vicarious traumatization for a wide range of
trauma workers. Each chapter addresses a particular worker
population or strategy for addressing the negative impact of
trauma work on the helper.

Skills Training Manual for Treating Borderline Personality Disorder by
Marsha Linehan (Guilford, 1993)

Given its name, readers may be surprised to discover several
excellent worksheets and discussions of mindfulness and distress
tolerance techniques in this workbook. The worksheets include
feeling topics, core mindfulness skills, and a list of 176 "Adult
Pleasant Events." These worksheets are helpful for personal use
or for group interventions.

*Trauma and the Therapist: Countertransference and Vicarious Trau-
matization in Psychotherapy with Incest Survivors* by Laurie
Anne Pearlman and Karen W. Saakvitne (Norton, 1995)

A comprehensive exploration of the therapist's role in trauma
therapies. The book looks at what therapists bring to therapy
relationships with survivor clients and how these therapies
change the therapist. It integrates trauma theory and therapy
with psychoanalytic theory. Useful for all who work with survivors or perpetrators.

Vicarious Traumatization I: The Pain of Empathy and *Vicarious Traumatization II: Transforming the Pain,* a videotape set with Laurie Pearlman, Kay Saakvitne, and others (Cavalcade Videos [1-800-345-5530], 1995)

Nine clinicians share their experiences of VT. Powerful and immediate descriptions of both the negative impact of trauma work on the helper and ways of transforming it.

Wellness at Work: Building Resilience to Job Stress by Valerie O'Hara, Ph.D. (New Harbinger, 1995)

A useful handbook on addressing general work stress. Many sound self-care strategies, including physical exercises, time management, stress reduction exercises and more.

The Woman's Comfort Book: A Self Nurturing Guide for Restoring Balance in Your Life and *The Couple's Comfort Book: A Creative Guide for Renewing Passion, Pleasure, and Commitment* by Jennifer Louden (HarperSanFrancisco, 1992, 1994)

Outstanding resources for women and men seeking to increase comfort in their lives. Chock-full of suggestions and encouragement for women's and couple's self-nurturing. Offers short concise chapters with many specific strategies and practical suggestions.

TSI/CAAP Resources

Any of these papers are available by contacting TSI/CAAP directly at (860) 644-2541 or writing TSI/CAAP, 22 Morgan Farms Drive, South Windsor, CT 06074.

Abrahamson, D. J., & Pearlman, L. A. (1993). The need for scientist-practitioner employment settings. *American Psychologist, 48,* 59–60.

Abrahamson, D. A., & Saakvitne, K. W. (in press). Quality management in practice: Re-visioning practice guidelines to improve treatment of anxiety and traumatic stress disorders. In G. Stricker (Ed.), *Handbook of quality management and behavioral health.* New York: Plenum.

McCann, I. L., & Pearlman, L. A. (1993). Vicarious traumatization: The emotional costs of working with survivors. *Treating Abuse Today, 3*(5) 28–31.

McCann, I. L., & Pearlman, L. A. (1990, Fall). Vicarious traumatization: The emotional costs of working with survivors. *The Advisor: Newsletter of the American Professional Society on the Abuse of Children, 3*(4), 34.

McCann, I. L., Sakheim, D. K., & Abrahamson, D. J. (1988). Trauma and victimization: A model of psychological adaptation. *The Counseling Psychologist, 16*(4), 531–594.

Pearlman, L. A. (1994). *Vicarious traumatization: The impact of help-ing victims of genocide or group violence.* Paper presented at the Annual Meeting of the International Society of Political Psychology, Santiago de Compostela, Spain.

Pearlman, L. A., & Mac Ian, P. S. (1993, Summer). Vicarious trauma-tization among trauma therapists: Empirical findings on self-care. *Traumatic Stress Points: News for the International Society for Traumatic Stress Studies, 7*(3), 5.

Pearlman, L. A., & McCann, I. L. (1994). Integrating structured and unstructured approaches to taking a trauma history. In M. B. Williams & J. F. Sommer, Jr. (Eds.), *Handbook of post-traumatic therapy,* 38–48. Westport, CT: Greenwood.

Saakvitne, K. W. (1991). *Countertransference in psychotherapy with incest survivors: When the therapist is a survivor of child abuse.* Paper presented at the 99th Annual Convention of the American Psychological Association, San Francisco, CA.

Saakvitne, K. W. (1994). The Traumatic Stress Institute: A model for psychoanalytic psychological practice. *Psychologist-Psychoana-lyst, 14*(2), 11–12.

Saakvitne, K. W. (1995). Therapists' responses to dissociative clients: Countertransference and vicarious traumatization. In L. M. Cohen, J. N. Berzoff, & M. R. Elin (Eds.), *Dissociative identity disorder: Theoretical and treatment controversies* (pp. 467–492). New York: Jason Aronson.

Saakvitne, K. W., & Abrahamson, D. J. (1994). The impact of man-aged care on the therapeutic relationship. *Journal of Psycho-analysis and Psychotherapy, 11*(2), 181–199.

Saakvitne, K. W., & Pearlman, L. A. (1993). The impact of internalized misogyny and violence against women on feminine identity. In E. Cook (Ed.), *Women, relationships, and power: Implications for counseling* (pp. 247–274). Alexandria, VA: American Counseling Association.

Trauma-Related Assessment Measures

Deiter, P. J., & Pearlman, L. A. (work in progress) *The Inner Experience Questionnaire: A measure of self capacities.*

Life Orientation Inventory (1995). A measure of spirituality. South Windsor, CT: Traumatic Stress Institute/Center for Adult and Adolescent Psychotherapy.

TSI Belief Scale (1994). An 80-item Likert-scale measure of disrupted cognitive schemas. South Windsor, CT: Traumatic Stress Institute/Center for Adult and Adolescent Psychotherapy.